STRIKING IT LUCKY

A BIOGRAPHY OF PAIN AND RESILENCY FROM ERITREA TO ST. PAUL

For Johanna —
Thank you
for sharing
my Life Story
Frezgi Hiskias
God bless
you.
7/21/2016

FREZGI HISKIAS
WITH
WALLY WAKEFIELD

outskirtspress

DENVER, COLORADO

This Book Dedicated to:
My Wife Sihin Francois who cares more than she knows
And
My Sister Hiriti Hiskias & Brother-in-Law Tekle Fiseha –
They gave me a home and introduced me to learning

Contents

Foreword by Trudy Klassen

Laura Schroff quoted a Chinese Proverb in her book, "The Intangible Thread". It read, "An invisible thread connects those who are destined to meet, regardless of time, place and circumstance. The thread may stretch, or tangle, but it will never break." When I read that proverb and Laura Schroff's book, I knew that proverb applied to my relationship with Frezgi. In her book Schroff relates the story of an advertising agent in New York City, who befriends a hungry, homeless boy of eleven, who lives on the streets of Brooklyn. The story covers several years. Until the present when Maurice (the young boy) has grown. He now has a family of his own and the relationship continues.

Of course Frezgi wasn't homeless. As far as I know, he wasn't hungry when I first met him. But he was in a new country and he had a "hunger" of a different kind. Frezgi's hunger was one for knowledge.

I was an English teacher in the Roseville (MN) Adult High School Program (RAHSP). This program had been established to aid individuals who had not earned their high school diploma. It also offered the opportunity for students to prepare to take the General Education Diploma (GED) tests. Originally, people who had left school early, or had been removed from the education system as a result of difficulties, were the majority of those attending in my classroom. The RAHSP provided the opportunity for students to earn the necessary credits to receive a Roseville High School diploma. The RAHSP was especially effective for young people who had struggled, for various reasons, in a structured classroom.

Licensed teachers in the academic areas of Math, Science, English and Social Studies, provided a comfortable academic situation for students and older persons, who for some reason had not been able to attend high school, or had felt overwhelmed in a regular classroom setting. I sometimes felt as though I should have been receiving pay as a "Counselor" rather than an English teacher. In many cases I believe I learned more from my students than they from me. I was frequently amazed at the struggles so many faced. I so much appreciated the effort they were making to earn a diploma in hopes of providing a better life for themselves and their families. I look back and treasure the memories of my twenty-eight years in the program. During the early years of my tenure in the RAHSP, we dealt with only English speaking students. So the arrival of a few students whose first language was something other than English, presented a challenge to provide a different approach. It was among this very small group of students that I first met Frezgi Hiskias. He had been fortunate in that before he arrived in the United States, he had the opportunity to attend a British speaking school. As a result he spoke English quite well. Additionally, he had earned credits in that school. We were able to build on his earlier experiences and thus speed up his track to earning a diploma.

My supervisor used to tell me that I had a tendency to become a "mother" to many of my students. This mothering instinct certainly applied to my relationship with Frezgi. He was always so eager to learn. This is a characteristic that always warms the heart of a teacher. During the time that Frezgi attended classes, he lived with a sister whose apartment was some distance from the school. The long walk to and from school must have been very difficult. When winter came, I realized it would be nearly impossible for Frezgi to navigate through the snow and traffic in an attempt to attend school. In his own story you will learn about this issue. Frezgi had been injured in an accident in his country prior to his arrival in the United States. As a result of the accident, Frezgi walked with a considerable limp.

During this time, as Frezgi struggled through the winter months, many of us teachers commented that if more students had his desire and dedication to learning, we may not have jobs. Frezgi earned his high school diploma and went on to do great things in spite of many difficulties.

He is a man with a great work ethic and a large heart. Anyone who reads his story will realize that the United States gained a wonderful person when Frezgi came here. I had long urged Frezgi to write a book about his life's journey. I was excited when he called to tell me Wally Wakefield was assisting him in this endeavor. I hope, through this book, many readers will learn what an exceptional person Frezgi Hiskias is. I am honored to have been asked to write the forward to his book. I am proud to have been his teacher, but even prouder to be his friend.

1

A Life Changed Forever

The story begins for all practical purposes when he was born. Frezgi came into this world on July 15, 1964. It was the hard life of a nomadic herdsman/farmer into which Frezgi Hiskias was born. He was a treasure among the people who lived in the western lowlands of Eritrea. He

Frezgi Hiskias as an eight year old in Adi Baba, Eritrea.

was especially a treasure because he was a boy. It was a difficult life. A hard life, but a boy was a valuable asset. A boy would grow and become a part of the life of the folk who lived in the dry, sandy, rocky and mountainous regions away from the Red Sea. Frezgi would become an asset to the family that lived in the village of Adi Gaba-Mai-Chew, just north of the border of Ethiopia. A boy would be a part of the family and soon would be expected to do the work of a man. The work to become a man began at an early age. The man would be a part of the family that worked the fields and lived a nomadic life style. That was all the boy would know as he was raised within the family. As he grew there was little he was to know of what childhood had to offer. He would begin to be treated as an adult at the age of eight, or in some cases, even younger. He would learn the life of a herdsman and farmer. He would be expected to learn the art of making tools for the farm. The tools would be carved from the wood of trees.

When Frezgi lived with his family there were many trees and several large forests. Wood from several kinds of trees were readily accessible and in abundance. Rope could be fashioned from vines or trees, or the skin of animals or preferably from the bark of trees and other plants. Frezgi became especially adept at selecting the parts of a tree that could be formed into yokes and other farm implements for oxen used to plow the fields. He learned to study the trees and soon became efficient at not only making tools used in farming, but he was skilled at selecting tree parts and making tools for house-keeping chores. He learned when to cut the trees in the appropriate season so as not to be affected by insects which would devour the lumber if not cut at the proper time of year. He would learn to make plows — except for the steel parts which would be obtained from local blacksmiths — and the parts of equipment used as utensils around the house.

A family may own cows, sheep, goats and camels. All the animals were important assets. As such they were valuable to the existence of the family. They had to be protected from the wild animals such as hyenas and large serpents such as anaconda and other poisonous varieties which roamed the region of Eritrea in which the Hisakis family resided.

Life in Eritrea is a struggle. The climate is harsh. The land itself is harsh – rocky and mountainous. It is difficult to live. Life is an endeavor just to survive. The climate is hot. Always it is hot - especially in the lowland areas. While somewhat modern aspects of life are beginning to reach some cities and towns, for vast numbers of people change comes slowly, especially to the inhabitant nomadic farmers of Eritrea. Life among the people has existed, as Frezgi knew it, much as it did for centuries. Life was a struggle for one's very existence.

Frezgi's father Hiskias Kebte, age 83, plowing a field as he prepares it for planting crops.

Frezgi's mother Zewdi Teweldebrhan (left) and his father, Hiskias Kebte in a picture taken in 1992

Family life is dear. Children are a sought after commodity. There is work enough for everyone. But rewards for the hard work are either sparse or nonexistent. It was into this harsh environment that Frezgi was born.

Boys and girls in Eritrea are honed to the way of life into which they are born. It is taken it for granted. There is no other way. The chores are simple. They are delineated between male and female. Once a certain age is attained — as early as five years old — the way of life of the nomadic farmer is expected of a child.

If you are a boy you are expected to begin to learn to herd cattle and other animals. You will soon be expected to man a plow behind oxen. You will learn to grow crops and to travel long distances, both in times of plenty and in times drought.

If you are born a girl you soon will be introduced to chores such as cooking, carrying water — many times for long distances — and other duties which have been delegated to girls and women in rural Eritrea.

Life can best be described as semi-nomadic. Not only when the dry season is at hand, but during the rainy season, your life is interrupted to

A well located in the town of Adi Gaba that was constructed by Frezgi's father, Hiskias Kebte. It is still in use today.

go to the areas where crops to sustain you for the remainder of the year can be grown and harvested. Travel in Eritrea is on foot and always at a jog. It is near nonstop. Usually it occurs at night to avoid the blistering heat which occupies and scorches the day. The blistering heat during the day brings activities to a halt. If herdsmen are awake during the day a rest period during the warmest parts of the day is taken. It is not unlike a long siesta period that has been known to occur in countries south of the United States. From the villages and their homes the people venture many miles to eke out their meager existence. Groups of people would band together to travel from their home villages to where the crops would be raised. The band would consist of relatives and others from nearby surrounding villages. It would be easier for larger groups of people to share tending for the animals that traveled with them. It would also provide better protection against wild predators and any persons who may have intentions of pilfering from the nomads.

A pattern of life is formed that is based on the seasons. Life as Frezgi came to know was shaped by the seasons. Life was broken down

A picture of Frezgi's grandfather Kebte Solomon.
This was taken in front of his home in Adi Gaba.

between the wet and the dry season. If the wet season was long enough, it would help to produce the crops that could sustain a family through the long dry season that was sure to follow. Also it would produce the grazing land that would sustain the cattle for long periods of time.

During the dry season long treks must be made to find grass on which the cattle and other animals can feed. With a practiced eye experienced herdsmen will scan the skies looking for rain clouds. They will then venture to find the grasses which have been nourished.

A view of the small town of Adi Gaba from high on a mountain top.

During the dry seasons the cattle had to be trained to adapt to a different way of life. Food was in short supply. They would be allowed to drink only every other day. They would become weak and wish to gorge themselves on water. The herdsmen would search for water. It may be left over in ponds. If it was particularly hard to find, a well would have to be dug and water carried by hand to the cattle. This pattern continues without change year after year. The young animals would soon be trained to the new framework that would be their lifestyle during the dry season. The rainy season could be expected to return in late April or early May.

As a young boy Frezgi grew up in the small, rock strew, dusty village of Adi Gaba in which his father, who has reached the age of 95 in 2013, still resides.

Frezgi's father has an older sister who is nearing the age of a century. She is living with her daughter in the capital city of Asmara and may well be the oldest living person in all of Eritrea.

The daughter left the region several years ago and moved to Asmara where she garnered an education and now is a school teacher in the city. To even approach such an age as 100 is very rare. Especially because such a hard life takes its toll on life. For a person who is born into the life style of a farmer and herder in the outstretches of Eritrea the average life span ranges from 40 to 55 years of age. The father of the family, Hiskias Kebte, has survived all odds and is approaching the century mark in age. The changes which he has witnessed in the way of life he knew, have been near inconceivable. The constant wars being waged by many different factions over the years have wreaked havoc the population and the economy. Forests have all but vanished. The herds of cattle have diminished and in some cases all but vanished. Modern ways have crept into the hinterlands. Automobiles and trucks have become more common. Telephones and even cell phones are creeping into the culture of herders and farmer nomads. Through it all one constant has been the strife brought about by the continuous conflicts between the warring factions.

2

Kids Found Ways to be Kids

Frezgi was a boy not unlike others in the village of Adi Gaba. The dusty, rock strewn roads were his playground as a young boy. He would seek playmates and soon learned a game not unlike "One-A-Cat" baseball where there were just two bases - a first base and home. The game was also similar to cricket and called Shaquee (Shah-Kee). This was a dry season game and played during the resting times of the hot parts of a day. It was also played during the evening when you were getting close to your destination.

There was another game — Yahlel — popular among older boys. It was usually played during the rainy season. Yahlel was a game that was played by boys as they followed the herds or during resting periods during the heat of day. It was played when the animals were resting on the soft sand near a river after they had finished drinking. Yahlel was played with two sticks. A boy would climb on the shoulders of another and with a long scoop ended stick he would sweep the other smaller stick from the ground in front of them out and away from the pair. If he was successful the boy would have to carry him to the stick. If he missed the stick lying on the ground, they would change places. Yahlel was played while the herds were grazing. The boys could play the game as they followed along.

A third popular competition was usually contested between villages. The older boys and young men would square off in competitions

Camels drinking water from a shallow depression. The water is transferred into a shallow animal skin flask. Other camels on the side anxiously wait their turn.

against the youths of a nearby village in a form of wrestling.

Food preparation was a woman's job and also taught at an early age to the girls. The daily diet consisted of a flat bread — "kicha" — made from flour that was ground on a stone mill. A large flat stone would be utilized and the grain would be crushed by kneading a smaller stone into the grain and grinding it until it became flour. It was then mixed with water and prepared daily. The large, unleavened round, thin crust would be served with milk when available or with water and eaten while still warm. Obtaining water was also a job carried out by the women of the family. When they were away from their home village and working the fields during the summer rainy season, obtaining water was a near back breaking chore. While returning from the fields the woman would be gathering fire wood which they would carry to their home. Once there they would pick out the earthen pots and then go to the river to obtain the water. Earthen pots, skillfully made by hand and carried on the shoulders or backs would be utilized to carry water. Or possibly, flasks of animal skin that could be placed on the backs of animals such as mules, donkeys or camels who would tote the water to the home site high up the side of the mountain.

The precious water had to be carried from down below the mountain where a well would produce the precious commodity. Gathering of firewood was another task carried out by the women and girls of the family. When they were not working in the fields, keeping them free of weeds, they would seek firewood to be used for cooking. Or when at home during the dry season they would embark on trips to gather the firewood. Firewood would be gathered and heaped into high stacks that would be hoisted onto their backs and carried to where the food preparation would be carried out. A summertime hut was built high in the hills.

The precious cows and other animals such as goats and pack animals had to be constantly guarded against predators such as hyenas or the wild fox which were lurking nearby. Also, there were bandit groups roaming the hills from which the animals had to be kept safe.

Several members of an extended family or well-known neighbors would band together. Each would work their plots of land. In mid-October or early November, it was common for the food supply to become low. When this happened, the weak or sick cattle that may not make it through the season would be selected for slaughter to sustain the food supply for the nomads. Chickens were also plentiful and supplied eggs and food that would help sustain the family. Some wild food and animals may be captured and eaten for sustenance until the new crops, such as maize, could be harvested.

Then came the joyous time when the harvest would take place. Life changed as the harvest would be gathered. It soon would be that the nomads would return to living in their home village from whence they had journeyed. Once gathered the grain would be carried or loaded on pack animals and the week or two journey would begin to return to the life in the village. The travel time to return to their home village would vary. It depended on which type of animal was being used to carry the harvest. Though dependable in the dry desert conditions, camels were slow travelers. If they were used, the journey to the home village might well take up to two weeks. If donkeys were used to pack the harvested goods the journey could be shortened by as much as a week. Also, camels needed a much smoother path on which to travel than other pack animals.

3

Thirteen Would Prove Unlucky For Frezgi

At the age of thirteen— while on the journey back to his home village — Frezgi would find that his life in this world would change forever. The day began like any other. The group of 10 or 15 family members and villagers were on their way home. The pain staking journey from the summer growing region and the return to the village of Adi Gaba had been underway for several days. Frezgi and his close friend Berhe (BURR-hay) had been driving the small cows. As young boys they had been assigned the responsibility of the calves of the herd. They were following behind the main group of people and had just crossed a large river. This lengthy tributary becomes dry during the arid season but full, bank to bank, during the wet season. The main party had forged the river and Frezgi and Berhe came behind and were proceeding on their way.

A fairly violent thunderstorm which had been building up nearby, suddenly broke out in torrents of rain. There were nearby accentuating flashes of lightening followed by loud claps of thunder. The main group — as was the custom — took shelter under a nearby tree. Understanding of the imminent dangers of lightning being attracted to trees was not common knowledge among the farmers and herdsmen of Eritrea.

Frezgi and Berhi, with their small herd of calves, started to catch up to the main group. The group that was huddled under the tree yelled back to Frezgi and Berhe to stay where they were. There wasn't enough room under the tree to give them shelter. Frezgi and Berhe regrouped the calves and headed a short way up the hill to take shelter under a nearby tree. As they huddled close to one another to wait out the storm — as they had done on many occasions — the two talked about how close they were to being home. They recalled that it was just two more days and they would be back in their village. Frezgi had with him his father's rain jacket and as the water began to drip through the tree he reached out to Berhe to move closer. Berhe put his arm around Frezgi as the two huddled closer to take refuge under the jacket.

As the two friends sat waiting out the storm it happened. The lightning which had been crashing and crackling in the distance suddenly wasn't so very distant. The tremendous crackling and crashing was now there. It was upon them! The flash and crash is no longer recalled. Everything went black. The lightning had struck. It splintered the small tree under which Frezgi and Berhe were sitting. It struck and leveled the two friends knocking them to the ground. The crashing flash traversed the short distance between the trees to where the main group was huddled. It struck the larger tree and leveled many in the party.

Frezgi's father who had been off in the distance tending to the larger herd of cows and other animals was concerned that they would be driven back into the river by the approaching storm. He heard and saw the lightning flash and sensed the imminent danger. He hurried to the group and surveyed what damage had been done. He looked over the group and saw that his son and his friend were not among the larger group. He found they had taken shelter some 100 meters away. He and some of the other men went to the tree under which Frezgi and Berhe had taken shelter. There they discovered their worst fears were being realized. It was feared the Berhe had been killed instantly. Frezgi lay unconscious and because of the terrible burns which covered his body, it was at first thought that he also had been killed.

The bodies were recovered and moved up to the main group which had begun to regain consciousness. Many were trying to figure out what had happened. The bodies of Frezgi and Berhe were placed nearby. When Frezgi began to stir they realized it was only Berhe that had been fatally stricken. The cattle began to come around the bodies. It was as if they sensed the tragedy that had struck. A small enclosure was made to protect and keep the animals away from Berhe. The cattle huddled around trying, it seemed, to understand and to arouse the body. The cows began to paw the earth with their hooves. They were sniffing and began to bawl as if they understood death and were "voicing" their discomfort in the only way they knew.

As some sense of reality, understanding and sanity crept back into the party, plans were beginning to be formulated. A fire had been built and Frezgi had been placed near the warmth. A coldness engulfed him. He made efforts to get closer to the flames and their warmth. He felt so cold that he wanted to roll over and into the warmth of the fire.

Meanwhile Frezgi's father, knowing the party would need help, set off for a somewhat distant village. He traveled all night through an unmarked and very dark section of the land. There was no distinct pathway and the journey was very hazardous through a landscape that was covered by sharp rocks and brambles which were covered with thorns.

As daylight slowly emerged on the shaken and disparaged party, wood was gathered and the making of a litter on which to carry Berhe's body was being formed and tied together. The litter was made with long poles. More poles were laced together to make a bed for the body. Berhe's body was to be placed on the makeshift platform. Four men — two at the front and two in back — would hoist the litter with Berhe's body between them. In this manner, when they were ready, they would be able to continue the journey. Also, early the next morning, Frezgi's father returned with a mule which Frezgi would travel on. Frezgi had many burns which had begun to blister into huge bubble-like sores that covered his legs and back. The burns were beginning to fester. It was determined that Frezgi and his father would travel alone because they could travel much faster than the main group which would carry Berhe, the cattle and the harvest. Frezgi was placed onto the mule and he and his father set off. As they traveled Frezgi — beginning now to suffer in pain from his burns — clung to the back of the mule.

Approximately a half hour from their destination, the mule decided to leave the pathway and venture into the thick brush. The area was one of brambles and with Frezgi rendered helpless and bound aboard the mule, there was nothing to do but cling to the wayward animal. Soon the mule was retrieved and brought back to the path. But the brambles had hit the blisters and they had burst as the branches and thorns had punctured the balloon like sores. Astride and clinging to the mule Frezgi began to suffer more and more pain. The burns had once more built into huge blisters and covered his torso — both front and back — and down both legs. His mid back and left hip and leg were particularly stricken. Throughout the terrible journey Frezgi's pain continued to worsen. There was nothing to be done but to persevere.

The two of them — Frezgi and his father — had set out about 6 a.m. in the morning. Traveling at a much faster pace than the main group the two arrived at the village of Maidema after 12 to 14 hours. In the remote areas of Eritrea there were no doctors or nurses and the people who lived on the fringes of civilization, knew little of medication. The practice of bloodletting was common. As yet, nothing had been done to alleviate the pain which Frezgi was enduring. In the village of Maidema there dwelled a man who was close to being a "medicine man". A person who practiced the art of healing with herbs. In Maidema, Frezgi was left to stay in the household of a distant cousin whose name was Yemanu Solomon.

Once these arrangements were made, Frezgi's father returned to the main group and Frezgi was left to face an uncertain future alone in the care of an aunt he did not know. Yemanu lived within a block or so of the man who was the purveyor of medicinal wisdom. From his home Frezgi could walk on a daily basis for treatment. For nearly six weeks he was cared for by the herbal healer, and slowly the enormous blisters healed and left his outer body.

As daylight began to break on yet another day of travel, the main group of the disassembled and distraught party set out once more to continue the trek toward their home village. The main group with the cattle and loaded animals carrying the harvest set off. The group was divided into two distinct parties. One would proceed with the body of Berhe while the other group tended to and drove the pack animals and the cattle. Berhe's body had been placed on the litter and was carried by four men. One each on one end of the two poles. Travel was slowed as they traversed and made their way through the rugged terrain.

Word of the tragedy traveled fast. Runners from one village in the area would spread the word to the next village and throughout the countryside. In this way the entire region soon heard of the adversity that had struck the Hisakis' family and party. The men would carry Berhe for a distance and then tire. Other men from nearby villages would take over. In this way the men carrying Berhe would go for a ways and as word spread of the tragic loss and disruption that had taken place, other men would hasten to meet the group and relieve the party carrying the litter. Unlike their Muslim brothers who buried the dead as soon as possible, these Christian folks felt the necessity of returning Berhe to a place where a proper burial could be performed. In this way the slow, near agonizing, journey was made one stage at a time. With relief coming in slow intervals, they made their way on their return journey to Berhe's home village of Adi Ambora - a short distance north of Adi Gaba - the home village of Frezgi and his family.

4

Healing Was Long and Difficult

It was sometime near mid-July when Frezgi arrived and was placed under the care of the person who was somewhat trained in the practice of herbal medicinal treatment. Not only was there no knowledge of anesthetics, but being in the care of a medical doctor in the outreaches of Eritrea in the mid 1970's was unheard of. Frezgi's wounds on the exterior of his body were administered to with a mixture of something organic in liquid form. The "medicine man" began to treat the sores which covered an extensive expanse of his entire body. Slowly, oh so slowly, his body healed. Healing came with as much will power on Frezgi's part and his belief in the power of God, as with the help of the medicine man. The sores that were visible on Frezgi's body healed, but many internal problems remained.

As Frezgi made his way to his home in Adi Gaba there remained much pain. The lightning strike also caused much internal damage as well as the sores which had been treated. Frezgi returned to his home in Adi Gaba but life as he once knew it, remained difficult and slowly turned to near impossible.

Frezgi began to have difficulty with his legs. His left leg in particular began to become deformed. A bone in the leg had stopped growing. As time wore on, Frezgi suffered more pain. His left leg began to become bowed as the small bone had suffered damage that hindered growth. Pain also began to creep into his back. More and more, as time transpired, the discrepancy between his legs grew. In the span of two or three years Frezgi came to be dependent on a cane. As the time passed he also developed breathing problems that had come about because of the damage to his lungs and his upper back. By the early 1980's the damage from the lightning strike had progressed through his body so that he suffered — in addition to the pain — with periods of severe feelings of cold. This feeling of cold was exasperated during the months between June and December. To make matters worse life became more difficult as people began to notice that Frezgi was "different". He limped. He was in need of a cane. He began to be scorned and even ridiculed because of his inability to function normally. Frezgi began to feel alone and abandoned.

5

Because You Don't See It, Doesn't Mean It Doesn't Hurt

Frezgi continued to heal and the sores from the blisters which had covered his body became less and less visible. But he continued to hurt inside. As he fought to endure the pain, he neither complained nor told anyone. It was not common or well accepted to be handicapped or a cripple in the hinterlands of Eritrea. As his leg became more and more deformed due to the problems of growth in the bone caused by the lightning damage, Frezgi withdrew from the games enjoyed by his peers. He didn't like the scorn and teasing that was increasingly occurring.

The pain began to increase in his back. He had difficulties breathing especially when he lay down. Frezgi began to fear that the lightning strike had damaged his lungs. Frezgi told no one, except his mother, of his internal pain. All the while Frezgi made every attempt to do his usual chores of herding and farming. He kept his secrets hidden from his father as he knew he was expected to continue to carry his load as a farmer's son. Frezgi continued — though with greater and greater struggles — to handle the heavy farm equipment and chores of farming. He still made the ventures to the farmlands. He still endured the struggles with the changing seasons. During this time Frezgi made infrequent trips back to the village where he was first treated by the medicine man. But these journeys began to be easier to put off because of his difficulty walking and the near constant internal pain he was forced to endure. It was about this time, some three years following the fateful day that he and his friend Berhe had taken cover under the tree seeking relief from the storm, that Frezgi's life took another turn that would again change his life forever.

Frezgi had a sister, Hiriti Hiskias, living in Addis Ababa, the capital city of Ethiopia. Hiriti heard of Frezgi's dilemma and made plans to take a trip northward to visit her family and find out for herself. After she heard of Frezgi's dilemma from a relative who came from Adi Gaba to Addis Ababa to visit her brother, she spoke to her husband, Tekle, of Frezgi's troubles. She asked if there was a possibility that Frezgi could return home with her. Her husband readily agreed.

Hiriti's husband, Tekle Fiseha (FEES-ha), whom Frezgi had never met, was born into a family whose father was a medically trained soldier in the Italian army. While Tekle was a young boy, his father had died. Tekle was taken in by an uncle who lived in Eritrea. His uncle was a farmer/herdsman and Tekle began life that was very much like that of Frezgi's. Tekle soon became disenchanted with his new way of life. He had an aunt — a sister to his mother — he knew lived in the City of Combolicha, in the Wolo Province of Ethiopia. Tekle made plans that were his secret alone to leave the difficult life of a farmer/herdsman. At about the age of 12 or 13, he fled from the harsh life he was living. He made his way by foot and with an occasional ride from the trucks which plied the route which followed the roads to Asmara and then on to Combolicha. When he arrived in the city he was able to locate his aunt who took him in and raised him as her own. While living in Combolicha Tekle Fiseha went to school. He was a bright student and was able to complete elementary school and went on to obtain a high school diploma. Soon he attended the university that was located in Addis Ababa and found his way into work with American Baptist missionaries. While working with the Baptist Missionaries he attended church. It so happened that Frezgi's sister attended the same church.

They met, found a common interest in one another and soon married. When he heard of the plight of Frezgi and his burdens of attempting to continue the way of life of a farmer herdsman, he was very sensitive to Frezgi's predicament. He understood how difficult this life could be and he felt that he and Frezgi had a lot in common. He quite readily agreed that Frezgi should come to live with them.

6

Eritrea is a Country Troubled by War

In Eritrea, there has been a long history of war that has been brought about due to many factors. There has been a constant struggle by powers that are envious of its rich and diverse natural resources including the near 700 miles of coastline along the western shores of the Red Sea. From across the sea came many foreign invaders. Many of these invaders were intent on the colonization of Eritrea. Down through history there have been groups of invaders from what is now Yemen, Ottoman Turks and Portuguese from Goa, Egyptians, and the British. In the 19th century the Italians sought to establish their interest in Eritrea.

Throughout the centuries, invaders have come from nearby countries in Africa such as Egypt and Sudan from the north and the west. And perhaps most troublesome, from the south, Ethiopia. But perhaps a major influence to the present day are the legacies left by the Italians.

Following the opening of the Suez Canal in 1869, many European countries were very interested in establishing coaling stations for their ships. It was during this time that Italy invaded Ethiopia and occupied Eritrea. At the turn of the century in 1890 Eritrea became a colony of Italy. In 1936 Eritrea became a province of Italian East Africa.

Strife and turmoil continued. In 1941, near the beginning of World War II, the British expelled the Italians and took over administration of Eritrea. The British control continued until a United Nations mandate in 1951 determined that Eritrea was federated with Ethiopia. This federation, in time, led to the annexation of Eritrea by Ethiopia and the country became Ethiopia's 14th province in 1962.

This was in direct deference to the authority under which the U.N. had established the federation with Ethiopia. The illegal action by Ethiopia brought about further stress for the Eritrean people. Under the harsh rule of the self-declared King, Haile Selassie, the country came under persecution and change. Because of an edict by Selassie, Eritreans were being forced to abandon their heritage. The Ethiopian emperor Selassie began to undermine Eritrea's autonomous government. The press was soon suppressed. Labor unions and political parties and all other democratic institutions were controlled by the Ethiopian government under Selassie's harsh dictatorial rule. Eritreans were soon obliged to adopt the Ethiopian Amharic language as well as pay tribute to the Ethiopian flag. Schools were forced to incorporate each of these harsh measures to make Eritreans assimilate to Ethiopia. Despite the frequent and regular outcries of the Eritrean people, the protests fell on deaf ears. Finally on September 1, 1961, the armed struggle for Eretrian independence was begun. The entire country was behind the rebels and their pursuit for independence.

The forces under the control of Selassie began to slaughter hundreds of thousands of Eritreans. An intense campaign was directed at dividing the Christians and the Muslims within the Eritrean borders. It was the dictator Selassie's plan to eradicate the Eritrean people. It was in 1967 that 500 civilians were massacred in the Barka region of the Western lowland area. This led to the first major wave of Eritrean refugees into Sudan. It was into this intense struggle and the horrors of war that Frezgi Hiskias was born. At the age of four, Frezgi can recall a series of horrifying tragedies in which an entire nearby village of Jihan was destroyed. The village was one of grass huts. In the darkness of late night a fire was begun with the wind at its back. It soon engulfed the entire village and its people. Eventually the Eritrean rebels, with assistance of the Ethiopian Communist troops, were able to overthrow Selassie. He was captured and killed by these forces in 1975. During these tumultuous times Frezgi was growing and was a witness to the many cruelties brought to his people. The Communists then took over control of Eritrea. At first the Eritrean people welcomed the change in government. However it was not long, under the directions of the dictatorial leadership 17-year rule of Megngistu Hailemariam that conditions deteriorated to a point of being worse than under Haile Selassie. It was during this time that countless more people were massacred. More Eritreans were being terminated under the Communist rule than under the long tenure of Selassie. The people found life under such a rule was not any better. It soon became much more bitter as the people of Eritrea were forced to endure severe hardships and more drastic life changes. Life in Eritrea under the Communistic rule and President Megngistu Hailemarianu lasted 17 years and was very harsh. It was widely believed the Communist plan was to eradicate the Eretrian people. Many Eretrian people were killed in what was considered cruel and uncivilized methods. Because of the cruel and inhumane treatment, many thousands of Eritreans began the long and hazardous near 600 miles journey into Sudan.

It was during the times of the harsh treatment in Ethiopia and the political mistreatment in Eritrea that Frezgi's oldest sister, Meaza Hiskias-Habtemariam, and her four children, made the journey on foot to Sudan to escape the cruelties. The dangerous trek took them westward through the rugged mountainous countryside and across desert terrain to escape the Communist rule, to Khartoum, Sudan. The trek from Adi Baba was made by walking. Several individuals — usually a small group of five to ten persons — would hire a paid guide to be safely guided through the dangers. The guide had knowledge of the whereabouts of the enemy troops. He was very concerned for his safety, as well as the safety of the people he was guiding. The walk was made in the darkness of night to avoid the scorching heat of the day. It was well known that if the group were discovered they would be imprisoned. The fear of being captured was well founded because of the very great possibility they would be physically mistreated before being shot or killed in some other brutal manner.

Frezgi is shown in a picture taken with his sister Hakiser. She traveled to Sudan and now abides in Germany.

So, for near ten nights the group walked through the dangers as they traversed the mountains and traveled through the desert to the border city of Kassala, Sudan. From Kassala they were able to gain access to a bus. The journey from Kassala took some 10 to 12 hours ride on a dusty and over crowded bus, before they would arrive in the city of Khartoum, the capital city of Sudan. In Khartoum, the United States and several European countries had established an immigration policy to assist refugees from third World countries of Africa.

In 1980 Meaza — along with her children — immigrated to the United States. She settled in Minnesota. That became a critical turn of events in the lives of several members of the Hiskias family. In 1981 — with the assistance of several contacts with churches made through the efforts of Meaza and the refugee resettlement program — Tsgeroman, and her daughter, followed the path — first to Kassala, then to Khartoum, Sudan as refugees — that led them also to America. Five years later, in 1986, another sister, Letezgi, successfully traversed the same dangerous route and eventually settled in America, where they remain to this day. Another sister, Hakiser Hiskias, also made the trek and today lives in Germany.

As he grew, Frezgi became more adept at the life of a farmer/herder. Frezgi survived in a war torn country. Not only was life difficult and harsh, but the war was a constant under which one feared for their life. It became even more terrifying when Russian war planes would come to bomb the villages.

The planes created havoc as they attacked the open markets and the herds which the people needed for their existence. Many persons were killed as they ran for their lives in an attempt to flee from the horror from the skies. During these terrifying times many families fled from their homes and into the mountains. It was under these conditions, in the relative safety of the mountainous regions, that many children were born.

During the conflict the main target of the Ethiopian government soldiers were the rebels. The Ethiopian soldiers were not particular. They randomly killed tens of thousands of Eritrean farmers. They slaughtered woman and children. They killed the herds of cattle, sheep and camels that were needed for the subsistence of the people. It is no wonder that during these bitter struggles that hundreds of thousands of Eritrean people fled the country and became refugees. It was during these terrifying years that Frezgi's three sisters, their spouses and their children made their way to the United States.

Finally, after 17 years of fighting, the Eritrean freedom fighters, with assistance from the Ethiopian anticommunist movement, were able to overthrow and oust the Communist regime. In 1991, the Communist government and its leader, Megngistu, went into exile in the country of Zimbabwe. Eritrea then gained its independence through a referendum in 1993. It was through the turmoil and uncertainties of war that Frezgi had made his way to the United States and to Minnesota.

7

Relief by a Russian Doctor

At the time that Frezgi traveled with his sister Hiriti to Ethiopia in 1980, the country was under Communistic rule. After his arrival, and through the efforts of his brother-in-law Tekle Fiseha and his sister, arrangements were made for Frezgi to visit with a doctor. The

Tekle Fisha and Frezgi's sister Hiriti shown in a picture taken in 1987 by Dr. Coleman while he was visiting in Ethiopia.

doctor advised that Frezgi should be admitted to have surgery on his deformed leg. Following the visit arrangements were made for Frezgi to have his left leg operated on. Because the hospitals were overcrowded with wounded soldiers, and the bribery customs that were necessary, it took nearly nine months for Frezgi to be admitted for the operation. In the period of time it took for a bed to be available, the initial doctor had left and a Russian doctor, Dr. Valary, was in Ethiopia in a special role of assistance carried out by the Soviet Communist government. The operation by Dr. Valary would be an attempt to straighten his leg and make his life more livable. It was hoped the operation would allow Frezgi to become more mobile. The operation was accomplished in 1981. His left leg was straightened and a plate was inserted. The plate was held in place with screws that were implanted to assist Frezgi to begin to walk in a more normal fashion. When this had been accomplished, Frezgi — with the use of a cane — began slowly to return to a near normal way of life.

When his father passed away Hiriti's husband, Tekle Fiseha, gave up the life of a herdsman and moved to Addis Ababa where he attended a university. He studied and soon became a successful teacher. Tekle then became a Director of the Swedish Lutheran School in Addis Ababa.

During one of the conversations between Frezgi and Tekle Fiseha it was suggested that it was time for Frezgi to begin school. When Frezgi heard this, he was near astounded. He wondered how anyone who had never had a day in a classroom of any kind, could even think about going to what was considered a normal school. Certainly Frezgi had not gone without a learned way of life. He knew well the life lessons learned as he was growing up. He had previously thought he would become a herdsman and farmer. It wasn't that Frezgi was not intelligent, it was that at the age of 16 it seemed improbable and near impossible that he could begin attending school. At the urging and strong suggestions from Tekle Fiseha, Frezgi agreed to give school a try. Tekle Fiseha promised to help in any way he could. So it was that at the age of 16

Frezgi Hiskias became a student and another great change in his life was being formulated.

Soon — and with great effort — Frezgi began to adjust to a life of learning. He found he relished the challenges that his studies provided.

With the assistance of Tekle Fiseha and diligent attention to his homework, Frezgi soon found that he was rapidly catching up to his grade level. Tekle Fiseha worked with Frezgi and taught him at home in the evening. It became a great challenge as in addition to the learning process, because of his age and size, he had to endure taunts from the children and the teachers. The teachers were not to be doubted - they literally ruled with an iron hand. Teachers were able to mistreat students both physically and verbally. Frezgi was ridiculed by the teachers because they thought of him as nothing but a "Country Bumpkin" and a loser. This ridicule by the teaching staff continued on into high school. They acted as if they were the "king" of their own little realm. They treated him in an uncommonly, near viscous manner. Frezgi challenged the teachers who treated him unfairly. The teachers found it not

Frezgi (standing right) pictured with several eighth grade classmates while in a Lutheran School in Addis Ababa, Ethiopia.

Frezgi pictured as an eight-grader while attending school in Addis Ababa, Ethiopia

within their way of life to be challenged by any student despite how they treated a particular individual. Frezgi made the best of the taunting and the mistreatment he suffered on a daily basis. In spite of the disenchantment he felt, he proved to be a bright student who became a dedicated learner. With the continued help of Tekle Fiseha, Frezgi was able to learn enough to be able, by 1986, to pass tests equivalent to a tenth grade level.

While the life of a herdsman was a noble occupation, it was a difficult and challenging way of life. Amazingly Frezgi was able to accomplish so much in the way of an education that in the short span of just five years, he achieved much more than he could have dreamed possible. More than anything, Frezgi learned and began to cherish his time devoted to studies. He began to realize that he truly was destined to achieve something more in life than that of a herdsman.

8

Maybe No Appointment
Was a Good Omen

At the time that Frezgi was in school in Ethiopia, Mr. Al and Mrs. Betty Johnson, from Edina, Minnesota, were there and working with the World Vision Organization. They introduced Frezgi to Dr. Victor Smith. Dr. Smith was in Ethiopia doing missionary work as an orthopedic surgeon at the East African Leprosy Organization Hospital located in Addis Ababa. Frezgi had first met Dr. Smith at the Sudan Interior Mission (SIM) Church. Dr. Smith was curious regarding Frezgi's maladies. When he was informed of the plight Frezgi was undergoing and how it had happened, he asked that Frezgi make an appointment to see him to possibly plan a surgery that would aid him in walking. Dr. Smith suggested that he could remove the plate in his leg and put him on the road to enhancing his ability to alleviate his physical problems. Frezgi began the process of making an appointment.

Because Frezgi was not known by any of the staff members at the hospital, it was near impossible to make connections. There was wide spread bribery of front office personnel. Frezgi would make an appointment daily, but as often as he made an appointment it would mysteriously disappear. He would arrive to keep the appointment with Dr. Smith, only to be informed that the appointment no longer existed.

Always there were plausible reasons given, such as Dr. Smith had an emergency, or he was not in that day or some other concocted excuse. Someone had bribed the people in charge of the records and taken Frezgi's reservation. This process continued daily for a period of two or three months' time.

Finally, out of frustration, Frezgi took matters into his own hands. Knowing the route that Dr. Smith walked each day on his way to work, Frezgi arose very early one morning and made his way to wait for Dr. Smith to pass. When he approached Dr. Smith the man was startled to see Frezgi. He asked where he had been. "I thought I told you to make a reservation?" he inquired. Frezgi explained what had been taking place. He told how, each day, he had been making appointments only to be told when he arrived of some excuse as to why he was unable to see Dr. Smith on that day He was sent away only to make another appointment that would not be available once he arrived to keep it the next day. Dr. Smith took him immediately to his office with the intent to work through the problem.

About this time, just as Frezgi was taking matters into his own hands and going to meet up with Dr. Smith, the fighting in Eritrea became more fierce and threatening. Dr. Smith then suddenly left and new doctors took over the hospital. The hospital was now filled with soldiers from the battles of the war. The hallways of the Black Lion Hospital were filled with the wounded. From outside the hospital the wails and cries of the stricken soldiers could be heard for blocks. Rampant rumors filled the city that, to hasten turnover in the hospital, amputation of limbs was easier and faster than treating men with severe pain and suffering. These rumors reached the ears of Frezgi. He heard that especially it was the practice of the many Cuban doctors who had come to the hospital who would recommend amputation. Fear began to creep into Frezgi's mind. He became convinced it may be more prudent for him to bear the pain rather than go through a scheduled operation that might end in amputation of his leg with the plate.

During these tumultuous times, Frezgi had continued to keep in contact with Mr. and Mrs. Johnson. The couple had returned to

Minnesota and had contacted Frezgi's sister, Tsgeroman. They were explaining Frezgi's plight to Tsgeroman and told his sister that they would be returning to Ethiopia soon to continue their humanitarian endeavors. Tsgeroman discussed the situation with her sister, Meaza, who had arrived in Minnesota two years earlier. She had come, along with her four children, through the refugee program by making the trip — first to Sudan — then to United States. Meaza had arrived in 1982 to join her husband, Solomon, who had made the journey a couple of years before.

Meaza was very much acquainted with the church and the process of refugees. She was acquainted with a person who was a friend of a Dr. David Sperry. Dr. Sperry had earned his PHD as an anthropologist. He had spent considerable time in Eritrea. Dr. Sperry's anthropological studies had brought him to Eritrea on several occasions. He spoke fluent Tigrinya and Amharic, the language commonly spoken in Ethiopia. He was very familiar with the plight of people from this region of Africa. It happened that Dr. Sperry was a close friend of a man named Dr. Thomas Coleman. Dr. Coleman was an orthopedic surgeon. Meaza hoped that through these connections, she could find help for her brother.

With the assistance of Meaza, Tsgeroman went to work with zeal. They met with people through the church. They raised money and made the arrangements to have Frezgi gain sponsorship to make the journey to come to Minnesota. The process is complicated to explain, but Dr. Sperry, when he heard of the efforts to bring Frezgi to the United States, interceded on behalf of the Hiskias family here in the United States. He introduced Meaza and Tsgeroman to his friend, Dr. Coleman, who was willing to perform the operation. Dr. Coleman then made arrangements with the Cambridge Memorial Hospital to perform the operation and provide the subsequent hospital stay free of charge.

Meaza and Tsgeroman had worked through the several churches and groups. The Colonial Church of Edina and the Bermachu family raised money to buy the necessary tickets for Frezgi. Sponsorship was obtained through the United Church of Christ located in Falcon Heights, Minnesota. By sponsoring Frezgi's stay in the United States, the congregation was providing assurances that he would be adequately cared for and not become a ward of the government. Having made all the necessary arrangements — the tickets were purchased — and the numerous details were carried out in order for Frezgi to make the journey to the United States.

Back in Ethiopia, Al and Betty Johnson had returned with the news that travel arrangements had been made for Frezgi to make the journey to Minnesota. Along with this came the news that both the operation and the hospital stay would be provided for Frezgi free of charge. The Johnsons had all the arrangements and papers necessary to make this a reality. Things had transpired in a surprisingly short time. Frezgi's life was once more about to undergo a drastic change. Frezgi's mind and thoughts were filled with doubts, trepidation and many questions. At the young age of 22 years, he felt very much unsure about what was happening to him and his life. Here he was, a farmer and herdsman from a remote village in Eritrea, about to make a journey to a country and a life about which he could only imagine. He knew of the United States, but Minnesota? What and where was that? He was assured by the Johnsons that everything was in order.

Mr. Johnson accompanied Frezgi to the United States Embassy in Addis Ababa. There Frezgi applied for and was granted a B2 visa. Frezgi now faced the prospect of embarking on a journey about which his mind was filled with many doubts and trepidations. So it was, as the calendar approached another New Year, that from the scorching hot climate, Frezgi was about to embark to begin yet another soul changing, new life in America.

9

A Journey to Change a Life

On the night the journey was to begin, Mr. Johnson came to pick Frezgi up for the journey to the airport. While undergoing the many preparations Frezgi had to say his "Goodbyes" to his sister Hiriti and brother-in-law Tekle Fiseha. Frezgi was to bid goodbye to their three children, along with many relatives and friends. It was a difficult chore, saying farewell to so many beloved relatives and friends. It was Hiriti and Tekle who had provided him with a vast amount of kindness. They had given him a home. They had changed his life with learning. Now he was about to leave them and the security they had provided for the past six and one half years. He had lived with them and had become a part of their family along with their three children. At this stage in his life, Frezgi was about to venture off on yet another and perhaps more drastic change in his life than any he had yet undergone in his 22 years here on this earth.

A major difference in this journey was that he was to get on an airplane about which he knew little or nothing. He would leave the familiar surroundings where he could communicate with people in a language he knew. He would venture into an environment about which he knew little or nothing. He would make this journey alone. This trip he would make without the assistance of any who understood him, his culture, his language or the turmoil he was feeling inside. Frezgi, after being up early in the day making arrangements, bid his farewell to Mr. Johnson at the airport. At midnight on the night of December 30, the anxious and unsure traveler made his way onto an airplane with the unfamiliar name of Lufthansa Airlines.

The first leg of his flight took him to a city in Saudi Arabia by the name of Jeddah. After a short stay of about 45 minutes the plane once more rose into the sky on its way to Frankfort, Germany. The plane landed at approximately 7 a.m. Frezgi disembarked at Frankfurt, Germany into the strange environment and hubbub of a major airport terminal. Frezgi now faced his first of many hurdles. He had no idea what language was being spoken. Even if he knew, he did not know how to speak it and could not understand what he was hearing. He approached a member of the airport personnel and in his limited English, inquired as to which gate he should go to next. The person he asked was, luckily, able to understand his dilemma. After Frezgi displayed his ticket, he was directed to the proper gate where he would wait to board his next flight. Frezgi sat down to wait. It would be about three hours before he could board the next Lufthansa Airlines plane for a flight to London, England.

Upon his arrival in London, Frezgi was confronted with another problem. After displaying his ticket, he was directed to and put on a shuttle that transported him to yet another terminal. He was somehow made aware that it was from here his next flight would depart. It was now near 14 hours since he had left Addis Ababa. Here now was Frezgi in yet another alarmingly busy airport where he was made to wait, once more confronted with doubt of not being able to understand the announcements being made. He was also struggling with the physical weakness of being overly exhausted. It had been 26 hours since he had any comfort of rest. Additionally he was enduring a large amount of pain that continued to plague him in his venture that he hoped would help him find some relief. Despite an overwhelming need for sleep, Frezgi feared missing his next change of airlines and the flight which would carry him to yet further mysteries. In the London airport he paced. He was afraid to sit for fear of falling asleep. He walked the corridors. He frequently returned to where his flight would depart. There were, slowly, more and more people gathered at the gateway, to await the flight that was to carry him once more into what was, for him, uncharted adventures across an ocean he had only learned about in geography books. His sleeplessness continued to engage in combat with his anxieties of missing the plane until finally, after some five hours of fitful waiting and just over 31 hours of being awake, Frezgi boarded a plane he hoped would carry him to America.

Still however the ordeal of flying was not over. On the plane Frezgi was seated next to an East Indian woman who was next to the window. As soon as the plane reached altitude and without regard to Frezgi, she sprawled out and occupied near half of Frezgi's seat and went to sleep. Not wishing to cause a problem and being polite, Frezgi endured the inconvenience. To further compound his discomfort the window shade was open. As the sun began to rise it became light. The sun was brilliant in a cloudless sky. It began to reflect from the blue Atlantic Ocean. The reflection from the sea made its way directly into Frezgi's eyes. The near blinding sun shining in his eyes lasted for several hours. Because of his inexperience and lack of knowledge of airplanes, Frezgi was unaware this discomfort could have been avoided by simply closing the window shade. Because of this ignorance, Frezgi endured. Even though he considered the fact he may be permanently blinded, he said nothing. The flight was made from London to Chicago uneventfully — with the exception of the discomfort of the glaring sunlight.

As the plane landed, Frezgi slowly regained his sight, when he disembarked for the first time on American soil, he was still without sleep. Despite his near complete exhaustion, it took little time before Frezgi was confronted with yet another obstacle. Before he could enter the United States, he would have to make his way through customs.

In the customs line Frezgi met an African American citizen of the United States. What little English Frezgi knew, was the English spoken by persons from England. For Frezgi, it was near impossible for him to understand the questions with which he was being confronted. Somehow, but not without considerable frustration on the part of both parties, Frezgi pervaded and was eventually permitted to pass through the Chicago customs. He again made his way — asking questions in his limited English language and displaying his airline ticket — to his next point of departure. Frezgi was about to board yet another airplane. This however held the hope of being the final leg of his journey. Finally he made his way onto a seat of a United Airline flight to Minneapolis, Minnesota. One can only imagine the joy that awaited Frezgi when he made his way into the Lindberg Terminal in Minneapolis, Minnesota.

Frezgi is greeted at the Minneapolis airport by members of his family, along with many friends. These people were speaking in his naive Tigrinya and Amharic languages which were music to his exhausted ears. Also on hand to greet him were a crew from a local television station to record the happy occasion

On December 31, 1986, the eve of not only a New Year, but the beginning of a new and uniquely different life for Frezgi, he made his way into the Lindberg Terminal in Minneapolis, Minnesota. Awaiting him in the terminal were his sister Tsgeroman and her husband. Joy!

They had been waiting with nearly as much anxiety as Frezgi had endured on his long journey from Ethiopia.

The relief was near overwhelming. Here now were people who could understand and communicate with him in his own Tigrinya — as well as Amharic — language. His sister and brother-in-law were not alone. There were many family members and several individuals from the Eritrean community on hand to greet him. On his arrival following a sleepless journey of near 40 hours, Frezgi is greeted at the airport by many people. The group included persons from various church groups as well as family members and their friends.

People at the Colonial Church of Edina who were aware of his impending arrival, had notified a local television station, KSTP-TV Channel Five, of Frezgi's arrival. They were there to record the happy and momentous reunion of Frezgi with his family members and the entourage which greeted him.

The relief felt by Frezgi was near impossible to describe. It was difficult for him to imagine that now he could stretch and not be confined to a seat in a crowded airplane. He most desperately craved the thought of finally lying down in a bed to relieve the pain, anxiety and frustrations of travel which were now behind him. The group happily departed the airport and made their way to the home of Tsgeroman where he would rest until the time of his surgery.

In two weeks' time — a mere 14 days after his arrival in Minnesota — Dr. Coleman and his staff at the Cambridge Memorial Hospital performed the operation that would rid Frezgi of the plate that had been inserted those many years ago by the Russian doctor in Ethiopia. Following the operation and hospital stay in the Cambridge Memorial Hospital, Frezgi returned to Tsgeroman's home in Roseville, MN to recuperate.

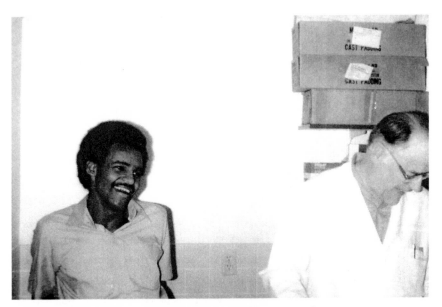

Frezgi and Dr. Thomas Coleman enjoy a light moment during a recuperation visit that Frezgi made to the Cambridge Memorial Hospital following the operation performed by Dr. Coleman to remove the plate that had been inserted several years earlier in Ethiopia.

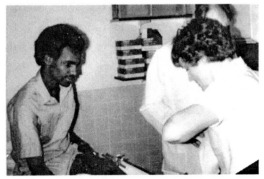

Dr. Coleman's nurse administering to Frezgi during the same visit.

10

A New Life Was Frigid

Frezgi arrived in Minnesota on New Year's Eve of 1986. Entirely new adventures greeted him. First, it was the cold of a Minnesota winter which he could not have even imagined from the weather conditions he had left in Eritrea where there were just two seasons consisting of wet and dry. Because Eritrea is just north of the equator and approximately halfway between the equator and the Tropic of Cancer it is very hot. The need for clothing worn in Minnesota were entirely unknown to Frezgi prior to his arrival.

Next, for the first time in his life, in the 22nd year of his life, Frezgi witnessed for the very first time something people in Minnesota take for granted. It was snow! Frezgi explained, "At first I didn't know what snow was. In Eritrea we had no word for it. It was completely foreign to me. The closest we ever came to snow, was if we had an infrequent storm which produced hail. We called it 'bared'. That is a word which means ice."

Frezgi arrived and soon the wheels were put in motion for him to visit with Dr. Thomas Coleman at the Cambridge Memorial Hospital. Dr. Coleman was an orthopedic surgeon. Things were happening that sent Frezgi's mind spinning. As a condition prior to Frezgi obtaining a visa to travel away from the country, Dr. Coleman had agreed to operate and remove the painful plate from Frezgi's left leg. The operation was performed on January 14, 1987, just days after Frezgi's arrival in the United States. The operation entailed removing the screws and the plate. He further stabilized the leg using cadaver bones to repair the deformity which had happened while Frezgi continued to grow, but the leg did not. Following the operation there was a six weeks hospital stay. This was followed by visits which entailed traveling the fifty miles between his home in Roseville and the hospital.

While Frezgi was in the hospital he witnessed the first snowfall of his first winter. It fascinated him. He likened the light and fluffy snow to cotton which grew abundantly in Eritrea. Soon he found the opportunity to actually touch some snow. "It was amazing to me to actually feel it," he said. "I knew that water turns to ice, so I expected it to be hard. It was soft. It was difficult to perceive. I found it hard to understand."

Frezgi recuperated enough and began to prepare for a new life of schooling. In the meantime, he was also working at a new job. However, the pain he still suffered internally as a result of the life changing lightning strike at the age of 13, continued to place challenges on his daily life. At times the pain which would plague him throughout the remainder of his existence, became near unbearable. Through it all Frezgi put his faith in God and thus was able to endure.

As he began his new life in Minnesota, Frezgi continued to live with his sister's family. He met with the many church people who had provided the financing necessary to make his journey into this new and demanding life possible. One of those persons was Roland Ehrenberg. Ehrenberg lived in Minneapolis but had an extended family who lived in nearby Wisconsin. All became truly great benefactors. To this day Frezgi thinks of Roland as his mentor. He remains one his closest friends. Through Ehrenberg and his many kind friends, it was suggested that Frezgi further his education.

11

Soon It Was Back To School

Frezgi began to pursue a new educational adventure after moving to Roseville, Minnesota to live with his sister. There he came in contact for the first time with teachers involved with education in the United States. While he was recovering from the operation by Dr. Coleman, a couple of Eritrean friends, Stefanos Dago and Kidane Gebray, came to visit. Frezgi asked them about continuing his education. Further discussion led them to suggest looking in the telephone "Yellow Pages" for Adult Education possibilities. Frezgi took their advice and there he found the Roseville Adult Education program listed. He called and explained his many problems, such as his age of 22, not having a visa to apply for education and having limited English. He was advised to come and take assessment tests in English and Mathematics.

As he began his quest for further education through the Roseville School System, he met Mrs. Trudy Klassen, an English teacher in the Roseville Adult Education program. Frezgi found that learning was possible at his own pace because the classes were one-on-one. Assignments were given and, when completed, the instructor discussed with each individual the work on the completed assignments. Mrs. Klassen became a friend and mentor and assisted him through the difficult adjustment period and then through the successful completion of his studies and gaining his High School Diploma.

In a picture taken in 1989 a very happy Frezgi Hiskias displays the Roseville High School Diploma he earned while attending school in the Adult Education classes.

During this time, Frezgi was walking a distance of two or three miles to school. There were no sidewalks and when winter came, the distance became near impossible — because of the snow and ice — to walk.

At one point during his first stay in Minnesota Frezgi was crossing a parking lot near his home. A car was pulling into the lot and suddenly he slipped on some ice. He fell right in the path of the oncoming car. The woman driving had all she could do to stop just before she would have hit Frezgi. He had found a new respect for the hidden dangers of a Minnesota winter. Mrs. Klassen became concerned about Frezgi walking and the dangers he faced with the cold of winter, the traffic and no sidewalks. She made arrangements for him to be picked up by a colleague, Mary Delarlais, to be driven to school. He further made arrangements to have his brother-in-law drive him home from school at near 9 p.m. at night. These arrangements greatly eased the concerns of Mrs. Klassen.

The language complexities had been a blight to his understanding and caused feelings of inadequacy in his ability to coexist among American society. Throughout the many challenges, Frezgi turned to God and remained determined to overcome and succeed in his new environment.

It was about this time in his stay in Minnesota, that another experience with snow took place. A group of friends were embarking on a skiing outing to a nearby ski area. They almost insisted that Frezgi come with and enjoy a new experience of skiing in Minnesota. Soon Frezgi was fitted with boots. They soon were attached to skis and he was off. He didn't get too far. He had difficulties with the rope tow, at one point he was unable to get off the rope tow! Once he did make it to the hilltop, he fell on the "Bunny Hill". On another occasion, in this first adventure on the slopes, he found it difficult to leave the T-Bar. Frezgi explained, "I fell more than a few times. I found I couldn't stop. On that first outing, I became very wise to it. It was a very challenging experience. Because of my condition, I was afraid I would fall and hurt myself. That was the only time I have ever tried to ski. I knew it would be my last."

Frezgi continued to enjoy the challenges that school and learning afforded. Following his successful completion of his studies in 1989. Frezgi headed to the University of Minnesota here he enrolled in and was accepted in General College. There he was able to continue his quest for knowledge. While at the University his knowledge and love of Mathematics gained appreciation and during his freshman and sophomore he became a mentor in Mathematics as a tutor.

With this occupying his spare time, Frezgi continued to pursue his studies with a passion. In 1994 Frezgi was accepted into the School of Pharmacy. However an unexpected major surgery had to be performed to alleviate disabilities to his right knee. His recovery from this operation was long and very painful. This interrupted his pursuit of becoming a pharmacist. At this point, he had already earned enough credits in 1996 to graduate with a Bachelor of Science Degree in Health and Wellness. He had in General College begun his quest in healing and this has continued his desire to aid his fellow human beings to the present day.

After recovering from the surgery on his right knee, Frezgi returned to school at Saint Paul College, near the History Center in St. Paul. He studied with a zest for learning that had been instilled in him. In approximately nine months, Frezgi earned a diploma as a Licensed Practical Nurse (LPN) in 1998. Once he obtained a license he contracted for a job and began to earn a living as an LPN at the Wilder Health Care Center and the Episcopal Church Home of Minnesota. The pain he continued to endure did not deter him and he continued his quest for education in the health services field. From May 2003 through May of 2004 while working at the Episcopal Church Home as an LPN, he gained enough credits to earn a RN degree in Nursing with honors at Century College in White Bear Lake.

He wanted more, but his education ran into a stop sign when he needed time off from school to undergo yet another surgery. This surgery would entail the correction of problems of pressure in his head due to hydrocephalus which had come about because of the lightning strike which had occurred when he was 13 years old. When he was taking a preparatory test to prepare for the state licensing for his Registered Nurse (RN) he underwent an attack which rendered him blind. It caused much consternation and frightened him greatly. Frezgi underwent a surgery to implant a shunt in his head to relieve the constant and very severe headaches he was suffering. The pain he suffered was very much like a person suffering from migraine headaches except that Frezgi's didn't end until several adjustments of his shunt. When this was accomplished, he returned to his learning endeavors. He earned a license and became a full-fledged RN.

With his RN degree, Frezgi was determined to use his talents to aid people. His nursing degree has led him into the field of hospice care, providing aid to individuals in their "End of Life" journey. This is a natural fit for Frezgi, as he excels in providing understanding to the patients and families through his kindness and generous spirit. Frezgi became employed in Hospice Palliative Care at Our Lady of Peace Home, located in St. Paul, Minnesota. Though his pain remains near constant, he continues his kindness and understanding while caring for persons he knows are living their final days.

12

Pain Is a Constant Companion

Through his entire life that has followed the life changing lightning strike, Frezgi has undergone several operations and almost continual pain which has plagued his life and hindered to a large degree at times his abilities to function. With the pain pursuing him through much of his day while he's awake and not allowing him adequate sleep at night, Frezgi continues his daily duties maintaining an upbeat attitude which he passes on to the patients he serves. The pain is alleviated somewhat during the day because his mind is active, he is dedicated to helping and aiding others during his duties as a palliative care nurse. The operations he has undergone as a result of the near life ending lightning strike are more than what one would consider anything but normal in one's lifetime.

They include the first operation which he underwent while in Ethiopia. After undergoing that operation in which a plate and screws were implanted to straighten his deformed left leg, Frezgi underwent operations after arriving here in the United States. A summary of those operations and when and where they occurred include:

- 1981 Orthopedic Surgery to straighten his leg. Insertion of a plate and screws at Tikur Anbesa (Black Lion) Hospital in Addis Ababa, Ethiopia.

- January 14, 1987 surgery to remove the plate in his left leg and repaired the deformity using cadaver bone by Dr. Thomas Coleman in Cambridge Memorial Hospital, Cambridge, MN.
- 1994 Orthopedic Surgery to repair the right knee by Dr. Elizabeth Arendt at University of Minnesota. This entailed utilizing bone removed from the area of Frezgi's right hip.

At this time while Frezgi was a student at the University of Minnesota, his good right leg suddenly "locked up". He was unable to bend it at the knee. It was determined the reason was that while his problems with his left leg were so prevalent for many years, that the cartilage in his right knee had deteriorated.

An operation to solve the cartilage problem was scheduled. When this had been accomplished Frezgi again went through a period of exercises to regain use of his leg. The operation complicated his walking once more. As the years passed Frezgi was becoming more and more "tilted". His right leg became even longer than his left, due to the surgery to repair the cartilage in his right knee. This created further discrepancy in his balance. He became more tilted toward his left side. This further complicated his balance resulting in the pinching of his nerves.

- 2004 Neurosurgery to place a head shunt was performed by Dr. Gregory Harrison at North Memorial Hospital. The shunt was inserted to drain the accumulation of cerebral spinal fluid (CSF) within his brain.
- 2007 Leg Lengthening Surgery by Dr. Mark Dhal. His nurse clinician, CNP Shannon at St. Croix Orthopedics assisted with his recovery and follow up visits the clinic.

Frezgi began to have constant shooting pain from pinched nerves. The pain was shooting down his legs. It was realized that yet another operation to relieve the pain was necessary. An operation to lengthen the bones in his left leg was scheduled. Frezgi was being disabled once more as his bone was slowly undergoing lengthening with a machine that operated twenty four hours each day. This lasted about a month in time.

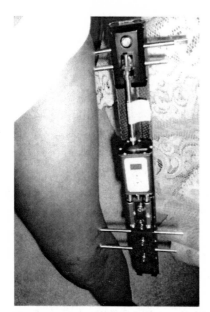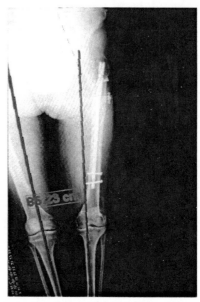

Pictures showing the apparatus (left) and an X-Ray (right) showing the pins in his left leg. Frezgi endured this machine for approximately six weeks as the leg was slowly adjusted to a new length.

This surgery would be very complex as his bones would have to be cut and slowly, oh so slowly, made to grow back together as his leg was being stretched with extender rods. Frezgi underwent an agonizing six weeks of extreme pain and suffering while the leg was undergoing this treatment and recovery.

During his early years of study at the university Frezgi endured having to stand in class with his back to a far wall because the pain in his back was so severe while in a sitting position. There was a time during a particular long test in 2004 that following the ordeal Frezgi became blind. His blindness lasted a few hours. After which, because of a piercing pain in his head, he was unable to lie down. He spent the night sitting on a couch. Through the entire night he felt the sharp and piercing pain. The next morning the sharp pain continued and seemed to penetrate his head. It increased if he even attempted to move or make an effort to lay down. The next morning he contacted his primary doctor. He explained what had occurred and requested an immediate MRI. His request was granted and Frezgi was administered the MRI and returned home. At about the time he arrived home there was a message from his doctor to give him a call back.

The news was very disturbing. The doctor informed him that he was a victim of hydrocephalus, a condition more commonly known as "water in the brain". It is a medical condition in which there is an abnormal accumulation of cerebrospinal fluid in the ventricles or cavities of the brain. A result of which is increased pressure inside the skull. It is a very serious condition which could cause blindness, loss of bladder control and even death. Frezgi saw a neurosurgeon and was told he should have immediate surgery to have a shunt placed in the right side, near the back of his head.

Frezgi was on the verge of taking the State Board Examination. The news of an impending operation was near devastating news. The news caused Frezgi further aggravation when he learned that it would be months before a surgeon would be available to perform the operation. He returned to his primary doctor who began a near frantic search to find an available neurosurgeon in the person of Dr. Gregory Harrison.

The surgery was accomplished on July 19, 2004 and a shunt was embedded in Frezgi's head to allow the fluids to again flow freely. The shunt that was installed is reprogrammable and magnetic in nature. When he again underwent an MRI to ascertain the reason for pain in his shoulder, the shunt was thrown off kilter. Frezgi has become frustrated several times and is fearful of passing through any magnetic fields — such as is used in airports and many public buildings — for fear the shunt will be disrupted and he will have to have it re-calibrated.

Frezgi has a strong belief in God and has stated, "I believe God has sent many medical professionals who have helped me over the past years of my life. It has been a painful journey. Through it all, I have gained strength from a merciful God whom I believe has had a plan for my life. He has kept me alive since the lightning so altered my life. (Psalm 124) If I believed that the end of my life was here on earth, it would have been not worth living. But my belief in and the hope of eternal life keeps me going."(1 Corinthians 15:50-57).

In 2007 Frezgi expressed his pain by writing a short essay describing what it is like to live a life engulfed in pain. He titled his essay, "Pain is My Life's Companion" and stated something to the effect: "Pain is the worst enemy one can have for any given period of time. Pain makes life very difficult. It eats at you from the inside and no one is aware of the fact you are suffering. Pain takes away your comfort. It takes away your sleep and makes your social life very unpleasant. Pain became a part of my life since I was 13 years of age. For the past 35 years I have dealt with pain constantly. It plagues me 24 hours a day for seven days a week. My daily comfort is disrupted. When I attempt to fall asleep I find it very difficult, because of the pain I feel. Only when I was sedated and heavily medicated during operations was I able to sleep for hours, then I realized that for most of my life I did not sleep well. During most nights I am awake every 15 to 30 minutes because of pain in my joints or in my back.

"This became a very normal routine for me and through the years, I have been able to somewhat endure and have learned to live with it. The past 10 months or a year have become the most difficult because of agonizing pain I have not been able to sleep for long periods at a time. Through this period only God knows how I was able to survive. My attitude and feelings about taking pain medications has changed, because I fear the effects of them will have an adverse effect on my life. At times the side effects of the medication is more frightening than the pain itself."

Frezgi has become allergic to many first line medications which are used to relieve pain. These allergies make relief from the pain nearly impossible. As a result of these allergies and his choosing not to take them, because of them making him nonfunctional, he has chosen to remain in pain."

He stated, "Because of the medications I became afraid of life and what may happen tomorrow as a result of the pain and the adverse effect of the medications.

"It seems as if I have almost given up a 31-year battle against pain, but because of my spiritual belief in God Almighty I have found a way to gain the fortitude to carry on.

"Because of my beliefs, I do not have to fear about tomorrow and my future. I know that God has a purpose in my life. I know he will get me through any hardship.

"Pain however is the worst and most difficult companion, but through the pain and because of God's mercy, I know it has no power to control me.

"The pain may fight me, but it will not overcome me. I know I will always be the winner through the power that God has given me.

"I truly believe that His Son — Jesus Christ — endured it for me when he died on the cross."

13

From Camel to Automobile

For much of Frezgi's life travel was always by foot. It was usually at a fast pace. The walk would take place early or late in the day. A rest period would take place during the blistering heat of the day. Walking was a normal way of life and one that, in the outreaches of that part of Africa, was what people knew and accepted.

Once Frezgi arrived in the United States, one of the wonders that confronted him were the number of automobiles that people in this part of the world took for granted. People, it seemed, felt an automobile was a necessity. Frezgi soon became enamored with the idea that an automobile was a way of life. It didn't take long before he felt that he must become accustomed to travel by automobile. He was determined to pursue the possibility to actually own one.

There was however a major obstacle. He had never before sat behind the steering wheel of a motor vehicle. Not only had he not sat behind the steering wheel, he had never before considered actually driving one. As a child Frezgi would occasionally catch a ride in a construction truck that may be hauling building supplies to a nearby village. Beyond that, Frezgi had little knowledge or understanding of how a motor vehicle operated. So it was that Frezgi was to be challenged once more here in America. This challenge would be the task of learning how to operate a motor vehicle. For anyone growing up in this environment learning to drive a car is taken for granted. There are driving lessons which one contracts through one's school connections.

Frezgi turned once more to his friends. His friends, particularly Abraham Tosfai, Roland Ehrenberg, Eyob Gebrekristos, Yonas Tekleab and Samuel Tekleab encouraged Frezgi to learn to drive a car. They became his major car driving mentors. They spent time with Frezgi. They took him to the Minnesota State Fairgrounds to give him driving lessons. For Frezgi the first several times were emotional and frightening experiences. He had many self-doubts about whether he actually could learn to drive a car. Frezgi had no such fear when it came to being on the back of a camel, a mule or even a donkey. Those had been a way of life with him and he could easily manage to allow any of those animals he knew to take him where he wanted to go when he was a boy in Eritrea.

Like most new driving students, Frezgi had difficulty coordinating the various levers and things to operate. Like most students he had difficulty coordinating speed. He would either go too fast or too slow. "I was afraid I might kill someone," Frezgi smiled. "I often thought about what might happen if I hit the gas instead of the brake" His teachers however, were understanding. Those same teachers were also full of encouragement. Finally they declared Frezgi ready to take the Minnesota State Driving Test.

He didn't pass the first time he took the test. The big day had arrived and he traveled with his friends to the former Federal Arms plant located in northwestern Ramsey County. Frezgi took the driver's test and failed at his first attempt. The road he was on for his test was unmarked with a line down the middle. Frezgi, on several occasions, had drifted across the center and thus became disqualified.

It was back to the drawing board. There were more lessons from his mentors. Again it was declared that Frezgi was ready. Frezgi was successful on his next attempt to gain a driver's license. But just getting his license didn't immediately give Frezgi self-confidence behind the wheel. It was close to a year and a half before Frezgi gained his confidence to feel comfortable enough to think about taking any long-distant trips.

The next step would be to find a car which he could buy. His first automobile was a Buick Regal. He then moved to a Chevrolet Corsica.

When he heard of the plight of three orphan children from Eritrea, he had them come to live with him. This caused him to consider buying another vehicle, one large enough to accommodate them. Frezgi explained that when he heard of someone — especially someone from Eritrea — who was in need of help, he had strong feelings for them. He felt compelled to do what he could to give them aid. The three young adults, two boys and a girl, were invited to move in to his home. They stayed with Frezgi and Sihin for a year. Frezgi then purchased a van to assist in conveniently driving the children who were now living with him. It now has been several years since his first uncertainties about sitting behind the wheel of a motor vehicle. After a year and half or so, Frezgi began to feel more comfortable and at ease when traversing the roads and byways of Minnesota and nearby states. He has become an accomplished driver and no longer has a fear that he actually might "kill" someone.

14

America Provides another Huge Challenge

Frezgi met Sihin in 1992 during the time that he was going to school at the University of Minnesota. At the time Sihin was working in a cafeteria located near the School of Dentistry. Frezgi and several colleagues would gather at the cafeteria to socialize and to study. Sihin had attended and graduated from the university located in Asmara, the capital city of Eritrea. She was now a student enrolled in graduate studies at the University of Minnesota. Other than they both were from Eritrea, Frezgi and Sihin did not have any relationship at the time. Over a period of years, they would occasionally meet at the Bally Fitness Health Club, located in St. Paul, Minnesota. The Eritrean community being close knit, they would also see one another at gatherings in which the local Eritrean community would be involved.

Sihin had an interest in music and had shared that interest with a friend. Sihin was musically inclined and had expressed a desire to become more proficient in her quest to learn music. This friend, Tsehaie Legese, unbeknownst to Sihin, was also an acquaintance of Frezgi. Tsehaie knew that Frezgi had brought with him a fondness of music from his native Eritrea and that he had several self-made musical instruments. Additionally, Frezgi is proficient on the guitar and keyboard.

One day, in 2001, Tsehaie suggested to Sihin that there was a possibility she could get music lessons from Frezgi. This was a somewhat underhanded method by which Tsehaie had felt that Frezgi and Sihin should develop something more than a platonic relationship. She suggested the two should meet and discuss possible music lessons. Here it should be mentioned while in Eritrea that Frezgi — because of his abilities to fashion workable farm tools and household utensils — had fashioned several musical instruments that were not unlike a flute or more accurate, like a recorder that is commonly found in American elementary classrooms. Once, while in Eritrea, Frezgi had fashioned a workable instrument on which a tune could be played, he also taught himself to play the instrument. As a herder and farmer in his homeland, Frezgi soon made several of the flute like instruments from the bamboo reeds which were abundant in the lowland areas. Once he learned to play these instruments, he would play music to soothe the animals during times he was tending them. His music also soothed his friends and family members as they listened to him play the songs he memorized and learned by ear. Frezgi brought this musical talent with him to the New World in which he now found himself. He began to experiment with new found materials. He soon found it was possible to make similar instruments using PVC pipe. As a result, Frezgi has become very adept at preserving the music from his boyhood days. He now plays during times when he finds it necessary to relax. Many times here in America, at gatherings of the Eritrean community, Frezgi will entertain his friends who long to hear the music of their native land. On many occasions he is asked to play his native music at church functions.

Armed with the knowledge that Frezgi was a musician, an unsuspecting Sihin called Frezgi to inquire about the possibility of taking lessons. The call was rather amusing to Frezgi. He strongly suspected that Sihin was not interested in learning how to play the "flute". That however, did not deter either of them from meeting to discuss the possibilities of furthering her "music" education. Soon they began to find more and more reasons to meet than just an occasional music lesson.

Through the years that Sihin had been here in the United States and in Minnesota, she had contacted an attorney to pursue efforts to become a permanent resident and eventually a U. S. citizen. Though she had been advancing moneys to the attorneys to accomplish this end, not much in the way of progress had been made. Sihin had put the matter aside and because of her dealings with the attorney, didn't give the issue of residence further thought.

One day Sihin made Frezgi aware of the fact that a certified letter was waiting for her to pick up at a U. S. Post Office branch in south Minneapolis. Frezgi suggested that he accompany her to the post office while she learned the contents of the letter. Upon opening and reading the letter, Sihin all but collapsed to the floor. The letter contained the most terrible news that any young couple could possibly receive. While in a state of shock, Sihin attempted to tell Frezgi that she was being informed by the U. S. Immigration Service that she was to be deported. She would have to arrange to return to Eritrea within thirty days! Her plans for continuing her education were to be stopped! Her life here in America would cease. What was worse, at this time there was yet another terribly harsh and bitter war raging in Eritrea. She was being informed that she would be sent "home" to a place in which she would almost certainly be killed.

The couple, which over the past several months were beginning to have serious feelings for one another, would be separated. This was a matter not to be taken lightly. Once Sihin returned to Eritrea as a deportee, even if she were to remain alive, there was little if any possibility she would ever be allowed to return to the United States. In that one moment — there in the lobby of the U. S. Post Office — they suddenly came to realize they were faced with the very real possibility they may soon be separated and never see each other again. For Frezgi and Sihin the situation was beyond dire. As they made the return trip home, they pondered the possibility they would be permanently separated. That unimaginable possibility caused much consternation for both. Frezgi and Sihin, who were on the brink of proclaiming their desire to become one, were now faced with the possibility of a life of separation.

During this ordeal they remained close. Frezgi turned to God for guidance. He cried. He prayed. He was near beside himself with worry and grief for all of three days. The world for both Frezgi and Sihin stopped. Their lives were turned completely upside down. In the Eritrean culture, life changing decisions such as marriage are not made quickly. In Eritrea it was still common for weddings to be "arranged" between families. Though more and more that custom was being abandoned, it was still very much the custom to gain consent between families of the young couple wishing to become man and wife. Now however, time was of the essence.

After three long days of contemplation and near constant prayer over their plight, Frezgi came to a conclusion. Something had to be done. It had to be done quickly if they were to have any favorable resolution to the enormous plight they faced. Frezgi made a difficult decision to go against all the Eritrean traditions which had been instilled in him. Both he and Sihin had a religious upbringing and the strong possibility — most influential and difficult for most U.S. citizens to comprehend — that Eritrean mores would be violated. But time was of the essence and Frezgi decided he would do something drastic. They would tell no one. He would marry Sihin. The couple would have to accomplish this as quickly as possible. That meant they would be married and not tell anyone. Sihin had two brothers who should have been informed. Frezgi decided they would be bypassed for the sake of expediency. Neither Sihin's brothers nor Frezgi's sisters would be told. So with two friends — sworn to secrecy — as attendants, they journeyed to the Ramsey County Courthouse, in downtown St. Paul and found a judge to marry them.

The young couple knew the Eritrean community would soon look at them with scorn. Even though they knew they had been legally joined, they realized they would be a viewed as a couple living together without the convenience or approval and having not been properly married. Such are the Eritrean customs. They realized they would have to rely on their faith in God to see them through these tribulations.

Frezgi had decided this immigration system that was seeking to deport Sihin had to be stopped. Having gone through obtaining his citizenship, he knew enough about the system to know that if they were to gain citizenship for Sihin they would have a better chance as husband and wife. It might be the only chance for Sihin to remain here in Minnesota.

An attorney experienced in immigration laws was quickly found and the complicated process of obstructing the deportation of Sihin was begun. Papers were obtained and filed. Court appearance were made. All the time the complicated process of overturning a deportation order was dreadfully slow. Time after time requests were turned down. As time passed, costs were mounting. But the determined couple kept investing in their future. As long as there was hope, or one more avenue to pursue, they were determined to complete their quest to keep Sihin here in Minnesota. On three separate occasions — in front of a panel of three judges — they met in Federal Probate Court in downtown St. Paul. Each time they were met with the disappointing news that their request had again been denied.

With each rejection they became closer to one another and to God. Their resolution, as well as devotion to one another, grew stronger. Sihin and Frezgi had a prayer group who met with them at their home every Wednesday for more than a year. Many things were a part of their devotions, but mainly it was Sihin's demise which was the main focus of their prayers. Among the regular attendees at these prayer gatherings were Pastor Girmai Mehretu, Mr. Taib Answra and Mrs. Tunsu Berhane.

The costs were now approaching five figures, but still they forged on. Finally, after three years and more than $12,000.00 spent, good news came from an immigration office located in New Jersey. Papers were to be forthcoming that Sihin soon would be allowed to continue to work and attend school as a legally documented person. Frezgi and Sihin were once more near overwhelmed with the most welcome news! Suddenly the desperations they had felt, the many hours spent in prayer and the passionate angst they had endured, were suddenly swept from their doorstep. They were free! They were emancipated from their doubts and fears.

One of the first acts of celebration on which they embarked was to go to the church elders of the Summit Eritrean Church. Once there, they made arrangements to have their wedding nuptials officially blessed by Pastor Ed Tedeschi, senior pastor of the Summit Assembly of God Church, in the presence of near three hundred people. The throng included relatives and members of the Eritrean community of the Twin Cities. This celebration was accomplished when Pastor Tedeschi announced to the entire congregation the course of action Frezgi and Sinhi had taken out of desperation — they had been married by a judge. They became "officially" married in their Eritrean community. The relieved couple could now continue to adjust to the life in Minnesota as a married couple and as accepted members of the community.

Frezgi Hiskias and Sinhi Francois are now a happy couple following their "official" wedding in which their vows were repeated in front of huge gathering, May 3, 2003, at the Summit Eritrean Church of Christ located in St. Paul, Minnesota. They are adorned in their native Eritrean finery worn for their "second" wedding ceremony. Following the ceremony they were accepted back into the Eritrean community as respected members who had done no wrong in their quest to be together as man and wife.

15

His Journey in Life Continues

Though the pain — since he was a mere lad of 13 years of age in 1977 — has not diminished, but rather has been a constant companion, Frezgi continues to feel lucky and committed to the life which he feels God has created for him. He daily gives thanks for his life here on earth and continues to be mindful of his path which provides care, guidance, love and sacrifice for those who find their way into his understanding graces. From his boyhood adventures, to the empathy of his sister Hiriti and her husband Tekle Fiseha, a new life in Addis Ababa, Ethiopia emerged. It was there that Frezgi found his way — with the urging and help of Tekle — into the formalities, at the age of 16, of a classroom. His rapid learning enabled him to overcome the ridicule and taunting of the other children who were enabled to goad Frezgi by intolerant teachers. While in Ethiopia Frezgi found his way into a hospital where his first experience with a doctor for an operation to correct his deformity and insert a plate into his left leg — followed by a four month recuperation in the Black Lion Hospital — that enabled his quest for a more normal life.

The hardships of life in Ethiopia continued as Frezgi continued to endure the pain before he once again transcended odds. As luck would have it, Frezgi made the journey to the United States to be with relatives in Minnesota. Arriving on the eve of a New Year in

Frezgi and Mrs. Trudy Klassen shown in a happy mood during a reunion of graduates of the Roseville Adult Education classes.

1985 — following a journey of pronounced anxieties — his pain was near forgotten with his enthusiastic relief of greeting relatives and people who could speak languages he could understand.

Frezgi was greeted by yet another new reality. In Minnesota Frezgi found for the first time in his life, snow and the cold of a Minnesota winter. Fourteen days after his arrival he met the kindness of Dr. Thomas Coleman and his staff at the Cambridge Memorial Hospital in Cambridge, Minnesota. Dr. Coleman performed an operation that removed the painful plate from his left leg. At the same time a cadaver bone was utilized to straighten the deformity.

Soon after and while he was still recuperating from the operation, another stage in the formal education of Frezgi's adventure was about to begin. While staying at the household of his sister Tsgeroman, Frezgi found his way into an adult education class in the Roseville School system. There he met Trudy Klassen who became his first and most important teacher in his new country. She understood his need to become more proficient in the English language. In time Mrs. Klassen has become a near "mother figure" to Frezgi. She has continued to be a friend to this day. Soon Frezgi felt the need and along with the urging of his friends, he began to undertake the travails of learning to drive an automobile. As Frezgi continued in his new life in America and despite his near constant pain,

Frezgi underwent a few other trials in the forms of surgeries. As explained earlier, it became necessary to have a shunt placed in his head. He also had a limb lengthening procedure which brought upon further pain and what Frezgi called his most painful experience.

Frezgi proudly steps forth to pick up his Bachelor of Science Degree at the University of Minnesota

A recap of Frezgi's hospital experiences which began in Ethiopia and continued here in America include surgeries in the years 1981, 1987, 1994, 2004, and 2007. His need, along with his strong inner desire to continue his education, has led him into a life of commitment to provide aid and comfort to others. This made it necessary to gain further educational pursuits. One such avenue helped him gain somewhat more independence when he became an undergraduate teaching assistant in mathematics while in General College at the University of Minnesota. Also at the University of Minnesota Frezgi earned — in 1996 — after transferring to the College of Health Sciences, a Bachelor of Science degree in Health and Wellness. He continued his appetite to gain more education in the field of health. He soon found himself in classes at the St. Paul Technical College. There, in 1998, he became a Licensed Practical Nurse. Then, at Century College in White Bear Lake, Minnesota, Frezgi's pursuit of learning earned him an Associate Nursing degree. As Frezgi continued to combat his pain, his resolute nature to succeed has led him into several places of employment.

Recapping some of these endeavors, his first experiences at the University of Minnesota as a tutor of mathematics, Frezgi moved on and became a nursing assistant — during the span of time from 1996 to 1998 — he became employed at the Wilder Health Care Center in St. Paul, MN. His service to provide for others caused him to move to the University of Good Samaritan Health Care Center located in Minneapolis, MN. These duties gave Frezgi his first experiences with the elderly as he provided essential nursing care, along with basic

Frezgi pictured with his wife, Sihin Francois, at the graduation exercises held at Century College where he earned a nursing degree in 2004.

Activities of Daily Living needs to nursing home residents. He assisted in maintaining comfort, dignity and the safety needs for his patients.

In the years 1998 to 2000, Frezgi moved and utilized his Practical Nursing experiences at the Wilder Care Center in St. Paul led him to the Episcopal Church Home of Minnesota in 2000. He worked there until 2004. While there, he was able to utilize his skills as a practical nurse and to hone his skills as a liaison between nursing home residents, staff, doctors and families. During this time and while he was extensively involved in study and finding his way from one health facility to another, Frezgi found time to marry and embark on a three year battle with the U. S. Immigration Department on behalf of his new wife, Francois Sihin. The newlywed couple endured the scorn of a few members of the Eritrean community, until they finally gained permanent citizenship for Sihin. Their future together in Minnesota was ensured.

Following the earning of his RN Degree and while he was recovering from shunt placement surgery in 2004, Frezgi received a suggestion from a staff member at the Episcopal Church Home of Minnesota, that he should consider applying for a position at the hospice facility at Our Lady of Peace Home, located in St. Paul, MN. This facility, formerly known as Our Lady of Good Counsel, is today operated by the Franciscan Health Community. It is in this palliative care facility that

This picture was taken in 2002 in front of the home where Frezgi was born.
Pictured are, left to right, Hiriti, Frezgi, Aunt Giday, Deres, a sister-Hakiser,
and some children.

Frezgi continues to ply his skills. He has become the "Charge Nurse" and sits with terminally ill cancer patients. He provides total patient comfort care, including pain control and symptom management.

Additionally, Frezgi acts as a liaison between separate departments of the palliative care team and patient families. Such things as physical, emotional and spiritual support are provided. His duties include being an advocate to the medicinal needs and care of the patients. He organizes such things as doctor's rounds and leads the palliative care team in providing the needs of the patient and their families. His duties include teaching symptom management skills and procedures to nursing staff who are new to palliative care procedures. He assists in the communication between patients, their families, and the palliative care team. In Frezgi's words, "I work in patient admission and in developing a plan of care for each new patient. We continually update patient progress with family and the care team. I teach and maintain patient comfort until the end of life."

Frezgi has felt a need to aid others in their need to gain experience in the field of nursing. He has endeavored to teach others. In 2007-2008 — while a full time employee at Our Lady of Peace Home — he worked at the Midwest Career Institute as an instructor to those learning to be nursing assistants and Home Health Aides. His duties entail teaching students the theory and clinical skills necessary to become proficient as Nursing Assistants and Home Health Aides. Additionally, he instructed his students in techniques of dealing with the American culture. In 2010 and 2011, Frezgi returned to the St. Paul Technical College to assist instructors with skills in laboratory tests for the Practical Nursing program. In 2010 he became a member of the St. Paul Technical College Practical Nursing Program Advisory Committee and continues to serve in that capacity.

Through this period of time that Frezgi has become involved with the needs and fortunes of others, he has also become involved in community needs. In this capacity he has become a language interpreter and document translator for the Immigration Bureau and the Minnesota Courts systems. He has clarified for hospitals and clinics the languages from both the Amharic and Tigrinya languages to English. He has assisted and continues to assist in breaking language barriers for others to understand since he began in 1995. Also, Frezgi is an advocate for individuals with medical and financial problems who may need help due to language misunderstandings.

From 2007 to 2009, Frezgi once again put aside his pain to help organize fund raising efforts for the Eritrean Community Center of Minnesota which is located in St. Paul. In the years 2007-2008, Frezgi provided foster care for three Eritrean orphaned teenagers. Additionally, from 2001 to 2010, Frezgi served at the Summit Eritrean Church of St. Paul as a church elder. To that end he has added duties such as a worship music leader. He also has been the Chairperson of the Media Ministry at the Medhanie Alem Eritrean Evangelical Church since 2011. Through this journey in life, Frezgi — in spite of the pain which has continually mounted efforts to deter him — has continued his faith in the power of God to assist him to endure. His belief in God as the "Director of his Destiny" has allowed Frezgi to endure his pain. If anything, the pain he faces has increased his efforts to make the lives of others maintain a more positive outlook no matter what misfortune they may face.

At this point in the summary of this man's life experiences, I would be remiss if I didn't make some personal observations. As we continued to interact over the months it has taken to document the account of his life, Frezgi and I have found a mutual friendship. My respect for Frezgi and his wife, Sinhi, has grown and has become very profound. One can only hope it will continue as we now continue our separate journey into the future. His beliefs in mankind as a whole have provided a positive outlook for all who have had the good fortune to come in contact with Frezgi Hiskias.

Epilogue 1: Kaleb Mehari

The real life ventures of Frezgi Hiskias would not be complete without some comments regarding his continued journey through his daily life. Frezgi has adapted his life to one of befriending and assisting others as he continues his duties while struggling with physical pain. He has committed himself to doing what is necessary to carry out his duties at Our Lady of Peace Hospice. Additionally he has added many other time consuming, but rewarding tasks, in his church and community, such as teaching and instructing others in his quest for purity and lifelong skills. Because of his modesty and the difficult task of finding words to describe his activities away from his daily duties at Our Lady of Peace Home, Frezgi has solicited a friend to explain what it means to know him.

One such person is Kaleb Mehari. Paraphrasing much of what Mehari has stated, following are his thoughts.

So, who is Frezgi? I came to know Frezgi through mutual friends more than a decade ago. I was informed before I met him how involved he was in the Summit Eritrean Church. Also, how much he has contributed to the wider Eritrean community. I learned how he was actively counseling, mending fences between conflicting parties and supporting his church and community initiatives.

After we met, I also came to know his wonderful wife Sihin. Frezgi, Sihin and I became close and personal friends. I then learned of his suffering from the excruciating pain brought about by the lightning strike that occurred when he was a boy tending his flock. It has remained amazing and inspiring to come to find he was doing all of the things in his life, without complaints and with no reservations.

If I hadn't come to know him personally, I would have thought he is as healthy as anyone can be. I have found that, because in his strong faith in God and the Lord Jesus Christ, he is able to put others before himself. That is a testimony in itself, without saying another word. Mehari continues, I remember a time when a Manager of our Accounting Department, informed me that her father was terminally ill and in hospice care. She mentioned the name Frezgi and said, "He knows of you." I told her yes, He is my friend. Then I said to her, "Your father is in good hands.

At times, Frezgi compassionately speaks of the people he works with and treats at the hospice care home. It cannot be an easy task to work with, and become attached with persons who are terminally ill and in their last gasps for breath, without complaining or mentioning the pain you are suffering. Yet, I do not know of anyone who is better suited to do this work than Frezgi.

Mehari turns to Scripture and quotes from the Apostle Paul who said in his second letter to the Corinthians, Chapter One, Verse Four, "Praise be to the God and Father of compassion and the God of all comfort, who comforts us in all our troubles, so that we can comfort those in any trouble with the comfort we ourselves receive from God.

Frezgi lives by this credo and I believe this is why he is able to touch so many lives, be it at his place of work, or in his personal life. As an example, a few years back, Frezgi and his family were actively spearheading a campaign to bring back to the United States, three orphaned children from Eritrea. After many ups and downs, the children were welcomed back in America. Frezgi brought them into his home as his very own. Though the children were eventually taken in by another family, Frezgi has continued an active role in their lives. One of the three in 2013 graduated from college and is bringing pride to his families.

EPILOGUE 1: KALEB MEHARI

Finally, Mehari goes on to say, Frezgi has a garden in his back yard. I don't know how he finds time, in addition to all the other things he does and despite the grueling pain, to manage such a wonderful garden with the many vegetables he grows. To someone who does not know, this garden is tended by someone who is in good health and has dedicated all his spare time to gardening.

Frezgi is indeed an inspiring man who puts others before himself. Despite his circumstances, he never complains. He is a good and dependable person. It has been a privilege to be able to state a few of my thoughts about Frezgi. I consider him to be a friend. He is a role model to me and to all others with whom he comes in contact.

-Kaleb Mehar

Epilogue 2: Dr. Meheretab Abraha

I feel honored to have this opportunity to write this statement on behalf of myself, my immediate family and I would include the members of the Eretrian community.

I have been asked to make comments about Frezgi Hiskias. I consider him to be one of a kind. Frezgi is a God fearing, wise, caring, kind and compassionate friend.

Perhaps he can best be described by a proverb which states, "A friend in need, is a friend indeed." Frezgi is not only a good friend to those who are good and kind to him. He is also a good friend to those who have nothing to offer in return. He is a kind and giving friend to those who have no other friends. Frezgi will assist and become friends with those who are forgotten or are deemed less important. He offers his kindness to those who suffer from being alone. He also seeks out those in our community who have "fallen off the radar", possibly due to physical, mental or health issues. Additionally, he will administer to those who are nearly helpless and are taken advantage of, because of their poverty, or those who have immigration problems.

I have had the pleasure of knowing Frezgi for some 15 years. We first met while we were studying at the University of Minnesota. I graduated with a Doctors Degree in Pharmacy. I now serve our veterans at the Veterans Hospital in Minneapolis, Minnesota.

However, I believe the biggest "School in Life" is not a university or college, but the largest school in life, is life itself. And in the "School of Life" Frezgi is one of the best graduates and at the top of his class! I feel honored to call Frezgi "my friend"! I look at Frezgi as being blessed with wisdom, grace, compassion and determination to — in all things — do what is right regardless of the consequences.

As a first generation immigrant, Frezgi has many time consuming and financial responsibilities. Like anyone, Frezgi, who lived a humble life in Africa, came to this country with much hope in his heart to fulfill his dreams. He has also carried a lot of determination in his mind to do what was best to make life better for himself and his family. Frezgi has paid little attention to his chronic back pain or the near constant pain in his legs and joints. He has shown disregard for the high personal price it has cost him. In his determination, he has placed his faith in God to assist him in his compassion for others. I find it difficult to describe in words the numerous wonderful things that Frezgi does for others.

But I will mention a few of the good deeds and acts of kindness as examples of the many things I have personally been witness to:

1) Frezgi is a bridge builder. The first generation Eritrean community in Minnesota — like any other first immigrant generation to this country — suffers from religious, social and political divisions. Each group builds its own walls around itself for many reasons. But I have witnessed Frezgi sailing unhindered in-between all. He approaches with love, care and respect. He delves into issues with the old, the young and even the little ones. Where others build walls, Frezgi is one of the few who build bridges regardless of religious, ethnic social or political divisions.

2.) Frezgi is a merciful forgiver, even to those who have meant to do him harm. When a woman betrayed her marriage vow and left him, Frezgi, unlike many of us, didn't resort to anger and resentment. He didn't to try to seek revenge. But instead, Frezgi forgave her. Not only that he gave her forgiveness, he indirectly helped her stand on her two feet and be free. Frezgi chose not to make her pay for the wrong doings she had done to him. In turn, the Lord blessed him with his wonderful wife, Sihin. She is also a believer in the Lord. Sihin is as passionate and compassionate as Frezgi. She makes it possible for Frezgi to do the many wonderful things he does. She stands behind him. She walks side by side with him, caring and encouraging him to do even more. Amen!

3.) Frezgi is a gifted speaker and communicator. In many of the social gatherings of our Eritrean community and at church activities, whether sad or joyful occasions, I have heard Frezgi sharing the word of God. He speaks not as a pastor, but as a humble, fellow human being. It is amazing to many to see how his words of faith, intermingled with the stories of his life, are so admired by old, the young and the little ones, all at the same time. I am not the least surprised that his words are received so well. He speaks from the heart and many times has more impact than those of ordained pastors or professional speakers. Frezgi carries his message from such a humble and wonderful heart that is filled with the grace of the Lord.

4.) Frezgi is a faithful believer and an un-surrendering soldier in the fight for justice. At a time in his life — about seven years ago — three orphaned children were removed from Minnesota by their adoptive parents. They were literally — in the eyes of many — dumped in Eritrea. Frezgi and his sister heard their cry for help. Though they were not related by blood, they had the faith and compassion to answer the desperate cries from the orphans across the Atlantic Ocean. Responding with love, hope and determination, they saw the injustice for what it was. With their experience and through their efforts, they were able to bring the children back to Minnesota. This was accomplished with unbelievable hard work by Frezgi and his sister, as well as many enlisted caring souls. When the three orphaned children were returned, they were welcomed into Frezgi's home as children of their own. It is difficult to imagine the financial burden, the social stress and most of all the huge immigration battle they had to wage to bring these — then helpless — children back to Minnesota. The problems they faced would have been more than myself, or more financially influential parsons, would care to undertake. Frezgi and Tsgeroman, armed with humility and a strong faith in the Lord — combined with their unwavering will to do the right thing — did not shy away from the well-armed Goliath, as did David with his faith. Like David, they too won!

5.) Frezgi is a compassionate friend of those who are in need. Once, when a young woman with a mental issue, ran away with her three children from an abusive husband in Atlanta, Georgia, She came to Minnesota, asking for help. In the course of several years, it was Frezgi and his family who became her advocates. In addition, Frezgi recruited members of his extended family, along with friends to assist in aiding the woman and her little children.

6.) Frezgi as a rescuer of those abandoned by their own. When political and religious unrest divided the Eritrean Orthodox Church in St. Paul in 2006, a former respected priest became a political liability to those in his own congregation whom he served. Overnight, he was literally dumped from his position by those who worshipped with him for over eight years. He was left suddenly to fend for himself with no salary for near six months. Additionally he was evicted from his shelter that was provided by the office of the Archbishop of the St. Paul Catholic Church. The Catholic Church had been providing financial assistance to the newly established Eritrean Orthodox Church in St. Paul. It was Frezgi who stepped forward to stand by this disenfranchised priest. He took him into his own home until he was able to find shelter for him. Without offending those who were responsible for the ouster, Frezgi, with grace, helped the elderly priest navigate the system and led him to a decent life. The abandoned priest lived with Frezgi and his wife for nearly four months. Finally, with Frezgi's assistance and help from a Ramsey County Adult Protection social worker, the helpless priest was able to find an apartment in which to live. Frezgi's help to the elderly priest did not stop there. He continued to assist him until he became a Naturalized Citizen of the United States. He continues his contact with the priest assisting him with his health care needs and the language barriers that continue to confront him.

As I stated at the beginning, many more things could be said about how wonderfully extensive and priceless an asset Frezgi is to our community. To the many others who did not have the opportunity to write a statement on behalf of myself and my family, as well as members of the Eritrean community at large, they would have felt blessed to be able to have this opportunity. Before I conclude, I would share with you, one more experience of which I and my family are the direct recipients and the beneficiaries of Frezgi's selfless generosity.

Last October (2012), my mother lost her older sister, our Aunt Bofta. Before her death my aunt was homebound, in part because of her age and other health issues. She was lonely, like many thousands of others who are living behind big walls of their apartments day after day. Too many times sons and daughters are overwhelmed with their daily and unrelenting busy work schedules, as well as other life demands to fulfill their duties to those they love. For several years before they moved, Frezgi and his wife were living in the same building. Even after they were no longer residents of her apartment building, they continued to be a blessing and God sent angels for our aunt. On occasions when I stopped to visit Aunt Bofta, she never failed to mention how great and wonderful Frezgi and his wife were to her. When my aunt became sick and was lying in a hospital bed, despite their busy schedules and distance of travel, Frezgi and his wife were constantly at her bedside to comfort her with their presence. They offered songs and prayers and shared with her the Word of the Lord. When the Lord finally called Bofta home, Frezgi and his wife were a blessing to the rest of our family. They turned our moments of sorrow into moments of joy. They helped us to celebrate her life. Because of their presence, our family will always be in debt to the care and generosity of this wonderful man.

I am happy and grateful that I have had the honor and the opportunity to mention a small portion of his abundant and ever flowing selfless love, care, compassion and generosity. At times I wonder how Frezgi is able to do all the things he does. But I believe he does these things not single handedly, but that his strong faith in the Lord fills his cup with grace continually. His belief in the supreme will of our God and His Son our Lord Jesus Christ have blessed Frezgi.

May His name be glorified and blessed for giving us a wonderful human being such as Frezgi. Among us, he is a big brother and an exemplary mentor to many of us. He is a true friend in deed, to those in need. Amen.

Acknowledgments

First —

I would like to say, "Glory be to God. My Creator, for his loving kindness and for the second chance he has given me in life.

Because I did not die that day of tragedy when I was burned by the lightning strike at the age of 13, I have lived a long life. In that life I have known the mercy and love of God. I have become to know that God has a plan and purpose for my life. I pray daily and try to appreciate life. I remind myself that each day is a day that the Lord has made (Psalm 118:28). I remind myself, I will try to make the best of each day for myself and for others. I know that only God knows what tomorrow will bring.

Secondly —

I thank Wallace (Wally) Wakefield and his children from the bottom of my heart. When he and his family were going through a difficult time at my workplace — Our Lady of Peace Home (OLPH) — he became willing to put my life story into a book. While at OLPH, I had the privilege of taking care of Wally's wife, Donna Wakefield, in the final days of her life.

One day Wally encouraged me to write a book. He said he would be willing to assist me. If it was not for Wally, this book would not have been written. May God bless Wally and his family!

ACKNOWLEDGMENTS

Thirdly —

I thank God for giving me my wonderful wife. Sihin Hadera Francois, is my life companion. She has been a precious gift from God for the past 11 years. She is my Angel who has filled void in my life in every way. Sihin is a true friend and my love. She has endured through much hardship in life with me. I praise the Lord for giving me such a loving and supportive wife.

My Family Members —
My Father Hiskias Kebete and my Mother Zewdi Teweldebrhan —

I must extend my gratitude to them for early in my life instilling in me God's love. Their closeness to God and their prayers, assisted me to be what and where I am today.

I thank God for my parents, along with my extended family from both my Mother and Father for showing me their love.

This extended family has supported me while passing through my painful life journey following my life threatening injury.

My sister Hiriti and her husband Tekle Fiseha —

It was these two who aided me to escape the harsh life of a herdsman I was leading in Eritrea.

They took me in and raised me, along with their three children, under the harsh living conditions of life under the Communist rule in Ethiopia.

These were times when there was scarcely enough to eat, yet they helped me obtain medical treatment and urged me to begin school. Because of them and their belief that I would succeed in school and in life, I am alive and was able to make the journey to where I am today.

My sisters Meaza and Tsgeroman and their husbands —

It was through their relentless efforts that help was forthcoming to allow me to be able to make the journey to the United States.

I must make special note of the efforts in particular of **Tsgeroman** and her husband.

The late Girmai Abraham —

It was through this man of wisdom and knowledge that I was able to learn in depth about both the Eritrean and American Cultures. Girmai was a great historian and one of the best communicators in the Tigrinya language. He had a deep knowledge of world history and geography.

The Centennial Church of Roseville, Minnesota —

I thank God for the members of this congregation who gave me financial aid when I was poor and living in Addis Ababa, Ethiopia. This aid was critical to help with my education and to pay for medical expenses during my hospitalization.

Mr. Habteab Teweldebrhan —

I thank my uncle for his persistence and hard work on my behalf to obtain medical treatment for me and to assist in me gaining my education.

The Swedish Lutheran School in Addis Ababa, Ethiopia —

This Swedish Mission Church School opened my eyes at the age of 16, to a whole new world. While in attendance I changed my thinking from that of being a herdsman to that of an academic student.

I would like to list several individuals at the school who had a special and unforgettable influence in my life. Those include:

Mrs. Letebrhan Gebregziabher who was my first English teacher. She told me I have great potential for higher education.

Kaleab Gorfu, Elias Gorfu and Yetbarek Wendmu

These men provided me with tutorial help in Mathematics and English. They also encouraged me during the first four years of my educational experiences.

Also, there was **Aklilu Milion** and his mother **Mrs. Tamre** who helped me obtain school supplies when I was poor and in need.

ACKNOWLEDGMENTS

Dr. Netsereab Tesfayohaness —

Dr. Tesfayohaness is much younger than I, but a loyal friend since my teenage years in Addis Ababa. During my elementary and high school years, he became a role model. He was an outstanding student.

Remember, I first began school when I was 16 years of age. I was one grade behind him and was able to use his textbooks through my school years.

We reunited again in the United States. I have continued to benefit greatly from his professional medical advice through my years struggling with pain, health problems and particularly when I underwent major surgeries.

In spite of his busy life working as an Anesthesiologist and managing his family life, Dr. Tesfayohaness has always made time to call and encourage me.

Mr. Gebrehiwet Weldeyesus and Mrs. Alem Kidane —

They needed me to attend to their son while he was in kindergarten and first grade during lunch hour at school.

During this time they provided me with transportation, as riding the crowded bus was near impossible because of my difficulty with walking. They saved me from a daily struggle of gaining access to the bus and the possibility of further injury.

Dr. Valery —

He was a Russian Orthopedic Surgeon at the Tikur Anbesa (Black Lion) Hospital in Addis Ababa who did my first left knee surgery. His expertise allowed me to be able to walk with the help of a cane during the several years before I arrived in Minnesota.

Mr. and Mrs. Al and Betty Johnson of Colonial Church of Edina, MN —

This couple worked for World Vision in Ethiopia. They helped me in numerous ways. Their efforts led to my being able to come to the United States and Minnesota. It was this couple who introduced me to Dr. Victor Smith.

Dr. Victor B. Smith —

He was an orthopedic doctor, working in Ethiopia, who made it possible for me to get permission from the Ethiopian Medical Board to immigrate to Minnesota.

The Falcon Heights United Church of Christ —

This church, located in Falcon Heights, MN, was a major sponsor to assist me in coming to the United States. David and Sheryl Redemacher were the key spokespersons to my being sponsored by the church. They were also responsible for coordinating the treatment and transportation from Roseville to Cambridge, MN where I underwent my first surgery here in Minnesota

Mr. Taye and Mrs. Wubalem Bermachu —

It was this couple who aided my sister Tsgeroman in finding a doctor and hospital that would give me free treatment. Additionally, this couple paid a part — along with the Colonial Church of Edina — of my airplane ticket that provided me with the means to come to the United States.

Mrs. Azieb Tekleab —

This woman introduced my sister Tsgeroman to Dr. David Sperry who was a friend of an orthopedic Surgeon, Dr. Thomas Coleman. After talking with my sister Tsgeroman, Dr. Sperry conveyed the fact that I needed knee reconstructive surgery. Dr. Coleman agreed to do the procedure.

Mr. Kiros Asefaw —

This man took all my documents, written in my native Tigrinya language and translated them into the English language.

Once they were translated into English the students at the William Mitchell College of Law were a huge assistance for me to obtain a "Green Card" and to gain resident status. Through them and the International Institute of Minnesota, located in St. Paul, I was able to negotiate my way through the immigration red tape.

ACKNOWLEDGMENTS

Mr. Fesehatssion T. Bein —

This man became my first friend in Minnesota. I lived with him, free of charge, at times when I left the dorm, while I was at the University of Minnesota.

Mrs. Trudy Klassen —

Mrs. Klassen was a teacher at the Roseville Area High School. I became involved with her when I applied for and was accepted into Adult Education. She greatly assisted and aided me in obtaining my High School diploma during my first encounter with formal education classes here in America.

Mrs. Klassen was an outstanding English teacher at Roseville Adult High School. While in her class, she became concerned for my safety during my first winter in Minnesota, when she found that I was walking a long distance to school, she arranged for me to have transportation.

Mrs. Klassen gave me much encouragement and it was her belief in me that prompted me to further my education. She has been a "mother" figure to me ever since.

Mrs. Klassen, along with members of the faculty at Roseville Adult High School — especially Mary DeJarlais, Dorothy Henricksen, Barb Cossack, Gordy Anderson and Paul Hamre — have provided me with a foundation on which I have built my career.

Mary was my history teacher who provided me with rides during the cold winter months.

Ms Mary "Kay" Kaloapolisi —

This woman was another selfless individual. She was one of the kindest persons I met during my early studies at the Roseville Adult High School. Since 1987 she has remained a loyal friend.

The Falcon Heights United Church of Christ -

This church, located in Falcon Heights, MN, was a major sponsor to assist me in coming to the United States

Mr. Roland Ehrenberg —

This man has been a mentor to me following my arrival in Minnesota. He has played the part of a parent and has made me a vital part of his extended family. He has given me loving kindness and extraordinary hospitality for more than twenty-six years. He remains one of my closest friends.

Dr. Thomas Coleman and the Cambridge Memorial Hospital —

He understood my need for reconstructive surgery. Through his influence with the hospital and their permission, he did my first and most important surgery here in Minnesota, free of charge.

He removed the plates that been implanted in Ethiopia in 1981. His influence at the hospital made it possible for me to have the surgery successfully accomplished free of charge.

Both he and his wife, Mrs. Elaine Coleman, were extremely supportive during my follow up treatments and visits that were necessary at the hospital as an outpatient.

The Hawthorne Dominican Nuns —

They have showered me with kindness, understanding and assistance that has enabled me to perform my daily duties as a nurse at Our Lady of Peace Home (OLPH).

OLPH is an "End of Life" care facility. It is a residential hospice that has been serving terminal ill cancer patients — free of charge — in their final days of living.

Mr. Shams Rahman —

I met Shams while in a Physics class at the University of Minnesota. He has remained a close friend to this day. While in college, Shams assisted me by carrying heavy books for me during a time when I was on crutches as a result of surgery on my right leg. We car pooled daily to and from school. He is a kind and respectful friend. His family also, has become my family.

ACKNOWLEDGMENTS

Dr. Meheretab Abraha —

A clinical pharmacist who has, since we met at the University of Minnesota, become a "brother" to me. He is a friend who is always available when I need him. He is kind hearted, a man of ideas and a great adviser in life. He is self-giving and will always go an extra mile to give aid to others.

Mr. Wosen (Yewendwosen) Tsegaw —

A good friend I met while in nursing school. He is an outstanding educator. He helped me to see my gifts and talents in many areas of life as well in the pursuit of nursing. From the time we met, he has been by my side in good times and in times of hardship. We have much in common such as playing music. Professionally we have collaborated training nursing assistants while we have been in the same institution. He is a man for whom I have high respect.

Mr. Mussey Mebrahtu —

I have high regard for this man and his entire family. We met at the University of Minnesota when he was a young man just out of high school. I found him to be a sharp thinker and an outstanding student. Through his friendship I have gained wisdom and a seriousness to my life.

Mr. Yemane Mebrahtu —

I thank God for this man. He has been a positive influence and supportive both morally and financially while his brother Mussey and I were students. We have traveled together and have had many good times for several years.

Abraham Tesfal, Yonas Tekleab, Samuel Tekleab and Eyob Gebrekristos —

These men all gave me valuable assistance while learning how to drive. I also worked with Samuel and Yonas at their family convenience store. They treated me as if I were their brother. Samuel was very financially generous to me.

Mr. Taib Ansera and Tunsu Berhane —

These two have been my spiritual mentors and advisers to me and my entire family. They have carried us in times of hardship and in times of happiness for many years. Thank God for their prayerful life.

Pastor Girmai Mehretu, Pastor Kibrab Issac, Pastor Mengis Atsbeha and Yosief Manna —

Through the teachings of these men, I have gained in-depth understanding of many strong biblical principles. Most of all I would like to acknowledge the Summit Eritrean Mothers of Prayer. Through teleconferences, we have as individuals and groups throughout the world, prayed each morning. Additionally, I thank God for those who have offered individual and group prayers for me while I was undergoing painful operations.

Mrs. Virginia Anderson —

This person is an Angel messenger from God. She kindly referred me to Sister Ann Marie of the Hawthorne Damian Nuns at **Our Lady of Peace Home** — formerly **Our Lady of Good Counsel**. This is a very special place that provides free of cost comfort care for terminally ill cancer patients and their loved ones. I have been employed as a nurse since being referred by Virginia in 2004.

Dr. Donald Erickson —

Dr. Erickson is a Neurosurgeon at the University of Minnesota. He alleviated the severe pain I had in my back through a percutaneous discectomy in 1990.

Dr. Elizabeth Arndt —

Dr. Arndt us an orthopedic surgeon at the University of Minnesota hospital who, in 1994, repaired my right knee. Additionally, she enabled me to fight the Student Health Insurance claim of a preexisting condition. She repaired my right knee with a bone from my iliac crust (right hip).

ACKNOWLEDGMENTS

Dr. Gregory S. Harrison —

Dr. Harrison is a neurosurgeon with a group of doctors at Millennium Neurosurgery. P.A. In 2004 he restored my sight by surgically inserting a ventricle head shunt. This operation was performed to relieve pressure caused by the building up of cerebral fluids (hydrocephalus, possibly caused by the lightning strike).

Dr. Mark T. Dhal —

Dr. Dhal is an orthopedic surgeon with St. Croix Orthopedics, whose specialty is limb lengthening. It was Dr. Dhal, who in 2007 performed an operation in which my left leg was lengthened by 4.6 centimeters. This restored my balance which had been deteriorating for some time. Assisting Dr. Dhal was Mrs. Shannon, a CNP nurse with St. Croix Orthopedics, who was an excellent health care provider during this difficult surgery.

The Hawthorne Dominican Nuns —

I would point out **Sister Ann Mari** for having the courage to hire me into their employment. There have been many others who have offered their support in prayer while I was undergoing painful limb lengthening surgery and recovery.

Additionally I give thanks to all the doctors and staff of **Our Lady of Peace Home** and **St. Mary's Hospice** and the many departments for becoming my family.

Mr. Thomas Cassidy —

Of all my colleagues, I would especially point to **Tom** whom I have come to depend on in each of my busy work days. I treasure the lessons I have gained from his gentle mannerisms, his humbleness and his selfless personality that have guided me in my years at **Our Lady of Peace Home**. I feel blessed to have someone so dependable in my work environment.

Mr. Matthew Stafford —

He has been my nursing Supervisor since 2004. I am very grateful for his willingness and patience in teaching me outstanding clinical skill. I appreciate him believing in me and helping me grow in leadership skills. He has been willing to share his wisdom. I will always remember the limitless support he has given during times in which I have been fighting pain.

Dr. Valerie Loichot

A professor of French at Emory University in Atlanta, Georgia who took the time and made the effort to edit the book as well as offer valuable insights into the content. Her assistance has been valuable to the success of the publication!

Laura Wakefield

Her expertise, diligence and assistance in formatting and editing has greatly enhanced the possibility of the book being published.

Additionally —

I would like to acknowledge several of my professors at the University of Minnesota — General College — who accommodated me. They allowed me, because of the pain I was in, to stand at the back of the class during their lectures. They understood my pain and gave permission for me to remain standing during class.

I would also like to acknowledge the many doctors and personnel who have assisted me on my lifetime journey that continues here in Minnesota.

Have You Been Struck by Lightning?

Most likely if you have been struck by lightning, you are no longer around to talk about it.

Frezgi Hiskias is one who talks about it in this book. As a lad of 13 years old, living in remote area of Eritrea, he was huddled under a tree with a close friend. The two were sitting under a rain jacket when the lightning struck killing his friend. This tale explains his suffering, beginning school for the first time at the age of 16 and his exploits from a humble beginning to his life's existence here in America.

The story is a fascinating tale of trials and adventures through his high school and his college degrees to his present day duties in a hospice care center.

It truly is a fascinating journey from the hinterlands of eastern Africa while sustaining a life of kindness and understanding empathy as he endures constant pain and resilience. Frezgi truly gives credit to the guiding hand of God for sustaining him through his daily efforts of serving humanity.

Wally Wakefield

The book is written by Wally Wakefield, a retired elementary school teacher of the St. Paul Public School system.

Wakefield has been a sports columnist for 34 years at the North St. Paul, MN based Lillie Suburban Newspapers.

He has written two other books — "On Wings of Wood" - A summary of the first 100 years of the St. Paul Ski Club" and a children's book, "The Best Toy Ever".

His experience in newspaper writing and public relations, as well as dealing with people on a daily basis, makes his expose of the life of Frezgi Hiskias explode from the pages of this biography.

Valerie Loichot, Professor, Emory University in Atlanta, GA

"I very much enjoyed reading this version of the book. I feel it tells a compelling story, with much decency and simplicity, which is difficult to do. It is an easy read that offers the reader a view of life and survival against many near overwhelming odds."

CPSIA information can be obtained at www.ICGtesting.com
Printed in the USA
LVOW06s0851300715

448213LV00001B/2/P

9 781478 749776